Flow Through Vessel

by Marnie Swedberg
www.Marnie.com

Flow Through Vessel:
How to Master the Habit of
Letting God Flow Through You

Copyright 2015
by Marnie Swedberg
http://www.Marnie.com

Cover Design by Paul Archie Teleron.

Layout Design by Surendra Gupta.

Editing by Nicole Alarie & Ellyne Uy.

Distributed by Lightning Source.

Published in the United States of America.

For more information contact:
Gifts of Encouragement, Inc.
2360 Corporate Circle, Suite 400
Henderson NV 89074
877-77-HOW-TO
877-774-6986
Info@Marnie.com
http://www.Marnie.com.

Swedberg, Marnie.
    Flow Through Vessel:
    How to Master the Habit of Letting God Flow Through You
            p.   cm.

ISBN 978-0-9829935-9-0

1. Christian Life.   2. Bible Study.
3. Worship & Devotion.   I. Title: Flow Through Vessel

First Edition/Book: 2015

There are numerous stories throughout the book. Most of the names have been changed, but the scenarios are real. Each is included to help you identify ways in which God is flowing through real people, just like you, every single day.

Acknowledgements

*T*his book was made possible because of the direct input and editing of the following 100 individuals, to whom I am eternally grateful. Thank you Nicole Alarie, Peggy Alberts, Ed Alexander, Sue Anderson, Michael Bahnmiller, Katie Bernard, Joan Berntson, Cherrilynn Bisbaon, Verna Bowman, Carole Brumley, Dave Buck, Zhumei Buck, Sherry Carter, Sue Carder, Wendy Cleare, Patty Curl, Mary Daniels, Linda Danielson, Emily Gail Dill, Janet Perez Eckles, Nicol Eichenberger, Judith Eick, Mindy Ferguson, Beth Fisher, Jonas Fisher, Nancy Fisher, Steve Fisher, Trey Foster, Vicki Foster, Carolyn J. Gage, Rita Thayer Garrobo, Nancy Kay Grace, Surendra Gupta, Mary Ann Hake, Patricia Hanson, Katy Harms, Paula Harris, Marla Hartson, Lynne Hartzell, Joyce Heiser, Susan Helweg, Karen Holmberg-Smith, Brenda Hostetter, Lori Hudson, Sharon Hurkens, Brenda Kilber, Carol Krahn, Kim Larson, Carole Leathem, Deborah Lynn Lewis, Gaye Lindfors, Cassie Lokker, Theresa Lovell, Susie Lucca, Michelle Maxwell, Amber McFarlane, Ronda McFarlane, Christie McLaughlin, Evelyn Mehlhaff, Marcia Mehlhaff, Tammy Milbrath, Civilla Morgan, Merindy Morganson, Tami Myer, Tamra Myrick, Mattea Oatman, Diane E. Owens, Joen Painter, Kim Ramiller, Sharon Riddle, Forshia Ross, Rosie Rygh, Donna Sallee', Jenny Schuster, Deb Scott, Carolynn Scully, Barbara Smith, Alice Spenst, Dave Swedberg, Doris Swedberg, Mark Swedberg, Paul Archie Teleron, Glenda Thomas, Brenda Thurman, Mary Townsend, Erin Ulwelling, Ellyne Yu, Stacy Walker, Verna LeRay Warner, and Deb Watson.

Table of Contents

Introduction

*G*arbage in, garbage out. Oxygen in, carbon dioxide out. Thoughts in, beliefs lived out. All this and more is happening without your conscious awareness, and it's affecting your life. The question is, "What is flowing through you?"

Most of us struggle with the concept of letting God flow through us. We've been fed a lie and, as lies go, it's a quality lie because it seems believable and includes an element of truth. The true part is that "God Is!" Indeed, God exists. The deceptive part is sandwiched in the middle: "God is not as good as He says He is." This lie feeds fear, breeds contempt, and leads us to distrust a loving God. Once there, we find it nearly impossible to yield our lives to Him.

God is actually far better than you can fathom, and His plan for your future is literally out of this world. His heart longs to be the love of your life. He wants to be your Source for everything. Being His flow through vessel is the greatest honor available to a human, and the benefits are awesome. They begin with peace that passes understanding and blossom into joy that thrives through the harshest storms of life.

I know this because God has personally walked me through fires and floods, a tornado, lightning strike, ambulance ride, head injury in the family, cancer in the family, sudden death in the family, business setbacks, sinking boat, car wrecks, a burglary, and more. God carried me; He still carries me. His life flows through me. He fills me with His peace and joy. He helps me and gives me hope. He allows me to extend His love to others—even during the worst experiences of my life. It's incredible!

I've seen God turn terrible tragedies into triumphs, and hopeless situations into happy surprises. I often have a front row seat for miraculous interventions and through every struggle, sadness, and loss, He's been with me. Even more, He gives me joy. The best news is that He wants to be all of this for you, too.

In these pages you'll find stories, analogies, practical applications, and quizzes to challenge your preconceived ideas about God and His plan for your life. You'll emerge equipped to live supernaturally, empowered by God, and funded with His resources.

The book is divided into twelve chapters, followed by a life application study guide, and ending with appendices. Either read the book from cover to cover, or jump around at will. In these pages you will:

- **Explore** the benefits of being a flow through vessel for God. (page 7)
- **Read the real-life stories** of five master flow through vessels to see how they walked through tough times, able to emerge full of faith, hope, and joy. (page 35)

- **Relieve any confusion** about God and life by learning to see things from His perspective. (page 47)

- **Reduce trauma** with the "4R Response," a simple process that yields immediate relief regardless of the intensity of the stress. (page 59)

- **Dream big, audacious dreams,** as you begin to understand how God sees you, what He doesn't expect of you, and how easy He's made it for you to succeed. (page 73)

- **Break free** and help others break habits and addictions, as well—gracefully, with God. (page 93)

- **Increase your trust** as you uncover the surprising reasons you may have found it difficult to have faith in God before now. (page 107)

- **Discover why** the Bible is important and believable, and why God loves it when you ask "why" questions. (page 117)

- **Gain confidence** to ask big. Of course, God must sometimes say "No" or "Wait," but as you explore His perspective, your faith will grow, and your life will change. (page 135)

- **Understand how God heals.** Investigate three specific processes Jesus used to heal blind men and the four ways God still heals people today. (page 141)

- **Dig deeper** with the Life Application Study Guide. (page 175)

When God flows His love through us, it's breathtaking. When that love flows from us to others, it's rewarding. Guess what?

When we get to heaven, He plans to reward us again for partnering with Him here on earth.

The fun part is that God cannot flow anything through you unless He first flows it to you. If God chooses to flow joy to someone through you, you have to experience joy first. Does someone need money? You have to have it in order to give it. It's a beautiful thing!

At least for me, there is no greater pleasure than letting God flow His life and love through me. My desire is for you to be filled to overflowing with His love, too. So, let's get going!

Section 1

Stop Trying Harder & Start Trusting More

Chapter 1
How to Live Beyond Human Limitations

She was whispering, the stranger on the other end of the phone conversation. She was asking if we could meet somewhere. She sounded desperate.

I'd been minding my own business, tending to my children, when the phone rang that night. Within thirty minutes I found myself at a restaurant, with a total stranger, listening to a sad, scared, confused woman share her life story.

She'd gotten my name from a relative who knew of me online, and had called me from her bathroom, where she was hiding from her drunk and angry husband.

I had no idea what to say or how to help. All I could do was listen to her while listening to God as He flowed words of comfort, instruction, and hope through me to her. Some of the words that came out of my mouth shocked me, and I remember walking out of her upside-down life, after two short hours, not knowing if she'd be OK or if I'd ever see or hear from her again. I just knew it was what I was supposed to do.

Over the next several days and weeks, whenever I wondered about her, I'd lift her up in prayer. It's one of my habits: To think of you is to pray for you.

To think of you is to pray for you.

And then, one day, it happened. I was coming out of a building as she was walking in. We nearly collided. To my shock and amazement, her face lit up like the sun, she gave me a huge hug, and she said, "Oh! It's you! I can't believe I get to see you!"

She went on to tell me how things had totally turned around after our meeting. Her husband, who'd been a drunk on the couch for months, had gotten up, found a job, and was participating in the family again. She gushed gratitude as she ran off toward her next appointment.

Stuff like this happens to me all the time as I yield my availability, mind, and body to God as a flow through vessel.

One day, when I needed to leave home for a meeting in less than 15 minutes, a random thought popped into my head. "Go mow the front lawn."

It was a crazy thought. It would take me nearly that long just to get the mower out and gassed up. I'd barely start mowing when I'd have to leave. But the thought was persistent. "Go mow the front lawn."

So, being a flow through vessel for God, I did. By faith, I chose to go mow the front lawn even though it made no sense to do so right then.

I'd taken just one pass around the external rim of the yard and was at the corner when I saw Sandy, a neighbor from six blocks up. She was biking and began to slow down as she noticed me in the yard. She pulled alongside the curb and said, "Oh, Marnie! Good! I needed to find someone who knew when AWANA was starting. Do you know?"

AWANA, which is a program that helps children understand the love of God, was scheduled to start that week.

As Sandy pulled away, waving her thanks, I walked the mower back to the garage where it would sit idle until that evening, when I'd scheduled time to do the whole lawn.

Then there was the day the thought came into my mind to check on a friend I hadn't seen for a while. Terry's well-being kept coming into my thoughts so persistently that I decided to swing by her house and check.

Upon arriving, I rang the bell. A frazzled-looking Terry answered the door. Apologetically, she explained she didn't have time to talk to me because she had 40 people coming for dinner in two hours and she wasn't near ready.

I said, "That's why I'm here! God put you on my heart because He knew you needed help. What can I do for you?"

Astounded, she immediately thought of three specific tasks for me to do. After an hour, she looked at me and said, "I think I'm ready to go take a shower and get dressed. We're done here. Thank you!"

Simple, silly, and inconsequential? Maybe. But these stories show what it's like to live everyday life as a flow through vessel: available to God with His love flowing through as He deems best.

Sometimes God's flow takes us way out of our comfort zone. One such experience started for me at 7 AM on a Sunday when all of a sudden I had this random thought, "Call Madison." The instruction was crazy. First, I wouldn't call anybody early on a Sunday morning. Next, I barely knew this gal, but what I did know was that she'd just had a baby. There was no way I was waking her up just because her name had fluttered through my thoughts.

Still, the voice in my heart persisted, "Call Madison."

After much prayer and pacing, and with sweating palms, I gave in to God and called. The transpiring events still take my breath away, but more on that later.

> God wants to flow to you, then through you, to everyone around you.

Being a flow through vessel for God is good for God, good for you, and good for others, too. Not only does God get His work done, but you get the benefit of being His tool, messenger, gift-giver, or whatever. Along the way, others receive God's gifts through you. In the end, God plans to reward you for your willingness to be used as His flow through vessel.

Definition of a Flow Through Vessel

The simplest description of a flow through vessel is a drinking straw. You stick a straw into a cup, suck in, and whatever is in the cup ends up in your mouth, delicious or not. The straw is the flow through vessel delivering the liquid from the cup to your mouth.

The more official definition of a flow through vessel is this:

**A flow through vessel is any
non-resistant conduit
willing to transmit a substance
from one location, form, or usefulness to another,
for its intended application.**

God used my mysterious mowing moments to personally invite Sandy and her son into a closer relationship with Him. He used my willingness to call Madison at a ridiculous time of day to meet a surprising need in her life. God wants to use you, too.

In the chapters to follow, we'll discuss the two main ways God uses us to be His flow through vessels:

1. **Direct Flow Throughs (DFTs).** These transport a substance, without changing it, from one location to another. DFT examples include straws, tubes, hoses and pipes. We are DFTs when God flows His love through us to others.

2. **Metamorphic Flow Throughs (MFTs).** These deliver the original substance only after a change to either its form or usefulness. MFTs include corrective lenses, the human body, and more. We serve as MFTs when God's presence through us changes the perspective or experience of another person.

> God is my safety net should I fall, my physician when I get hurt, and my heavenly home when I die.

As people come near you, like an elevator serving as a DFT, your influence takes their spirits up or down. At other times, like a purifying water cooler serving as an MFT, you have the opportunity to invigorate and recharge people who are spiritually dying of thirst.

God wants to flow to you, then through you, to everyone around you.

You Are Already a Flow Through Vessel

Until this moment, you may have been mostly unaware of what is flowing through you, but that's about to change. We are going to look at all types of flow through vessels from wind pipes to water hoses. Some will be straight forward, like the drinking straw, while others less obvious, like a pair of sun-glasses, changing the perception of the sun flowing through them, from glaring to a gentle glow.

As we go, we'll look at how letting God's life flow through us is so different from trying harder to be like God. Trying harder leads to frustration, guilt, and hopelessness, whereas trusting more results in joy, anticipation, and a close personal relationship with the God of the universe.

I used to try hard to be like Jesus. Now I trust hard and let God flow through me because that's the way He planned it to be. Oswald Chambers said something similar, and I love saying it like this: "No more sigh of sadness; only breathless expectation at what God is going to do next through my life."

On the morning I called Madison, I couldn't have known that burglars had surrounded her little house out in the country during the night. Her husband was out of town, so she was there alone with a dog and her baby. She'd called the police and was OK, but she'd been too scared to go back to sleep after the police left.

I couldn't have known she would welcome my 7 AM call or gratefully give me her newborn child to care for that day while she rested.

Madison's life story was another surprise, along with her numerous failed attempts to connect with God, and her longing to know Him.

All I knew were the two words, "Call Madison." Or, to be honest, three words by the time I argued with God about it, after which I heard, "Call Madison now!"

Sitting with this young mom in her living room, after she'd rested, I asked if she ever prayed. She said, "I pray all the time."

Sensing her despair, I asked, "Do you think God hears you?"

Her brokenhearted answer was, "I don't think so."

Marnie Swedberg

Maybe you, like Madison, have experienced God as distant and unavailable. I'm here to tell you, He is closer than your next breath.

As Madison nursed the baby, I explained how she could connect with God once and for all, inviting Him to flow His life through her from that moment forward. Madison said yes. She trusted Jesus as her Savior that day and she's been His flow through vessel ever since.

These stories are typical of how God flows through my life in basic, everyday ways, for eternal reward, but sometimes the process affects more than one life at a time. There was a weekend when I pinch-hit for a keynote speaker whose back went out the day before a women's conference. I was able to cover all my local responsibilities, be packed, and out the door toward the plane within a few hours, get the last seat on the last flight to the location, and use the system God had taught me to pull together four, hour-long presentations just in time to give each.

That weekend was breathtakingly awesome. I watched God move powerfully in the lives of so many women. In addition, He honored me publicly with the longest standing ovation I've ever enjoyed. It was such a spiritual mountaintop I wasn't sure I'd ever come down, but, of course, I did.

I've also lived through near-death experiences, financial setbacks, fires, floods, a tornado, lightning strike, and so much more. God, flowing His peace and provision through me, makes my life a joyful roller coaster ride, whether up or down.

As you journey toward becoming a master flow through vessel for God, I'm excited to share the concepts, benefits, and practical steps required to enjoy this new lifestyle of peace and eternal usefulness.

There are so many reasons to live life as a flow through vessel for God. Personally, I love the joy I feel as God flows His love through me to others, the fearlessness I experience with God inside me, and the willingness I enjoy to attempt things I'd otherwise never try. God is my safety net should I fall, my physician when I get hurt, and my heavenly home when I die.

It's a crazy, wonderful life!

As God's flow through vessel, I'm never lonely; instead, I enjoy a deep, loving relationship with God Himself. He is always with me, no matter where I am or what I'm going through. I have hope because I know He loves it when I give Him every last thing including my mistakes, missteps, and misspoken words. I've seen Him transform even my most hideous and embarrassing trash into beautiful, God-honoring treasure. I enjoy freedom to be fully myself because God knows me best and loves me most. I am encouraged to be completely vulnerable with God.

The habit of being a flow through vessel for God is easy enough for anyone, even a small child, to learn and master. There are just two steps:

1. Get connected to God, so He can flow into you.
2. Allow Him to freely flow through your life.

I had the privilege of getting connected to God when I was just four years old. I still remember where I was, who helped me understand, and why I made that decision. Since then, I've progressively learned to let God flow through me more and more, not trying harder to be like Jesus, but spending time with God, getting to know Him better, and learning to trust Him more.

It's a crazy, wonderful life!

One day I was driving around town, delivering invitations to a women's Bible study I planned to restart the following week in my home. I'd put together a route so I could visit each lady at the ideal time of day for her.

As I turned on my right blinker to go toward my first stop, I understood to go straight instead of turning right. I heard in my head, "Go to Pam's first."

This was a problem: I had intentionally placed Pam's stop at the end of the route, since I knew she'd be picking up her kids from daycare at this time of day. She wouldn't be home yet, so I ignored the idea and continued toward the right turn lane.

I heard the prompting again, "Go straight. Go to Pam's now."

This time I argued aloud with God and said, "She won't be home yet, and, God, I really wanted to invite her in person because she's been gone for several months. If I go now, I'll miss her."

But the prompting came again, stronger, "Go straight to Pam's."

I didn't hear an audible voice, and the clouds did not part. I saw no lightning nor did I feel any emotion in particular. I just knew, despite all logic, to go to Pam's first. So I did.

I turned off my blinker and drove the three miles to Pam's, confused, but compliant. (I learned a long time ago to let God lead me around, even when His instructions don't make any sense to me.)

As I came around a bend in her long, winding driveway, there was Pam in her pick-up truck coming straight toward me. Amazed, I inched forward until our driver's windows were side by side.

I'm not sure who was more surprised to see the other, but she was the first to speak. In a tone verging on accusatory, Pam demanded, "Marnie! What are you doing here?"

I grabbed the invitation and handed it through the window, explaining that I'd come to invite her back to Bible study.

She looked at me incredulously, shaking her head from side to side, and said, "No! But why are you *really* here?"

Taken aback by her intensity, I said more slowly, enunciating each word, "I came to invite you back to Bible study. We've missed you. We want you to come back."

Squinting her eyes a bit, she said, "So, you really don't know?"

Puzzled, I said, "Know what?"

"Marnie, today's my birthday! One year ago today, I sat across the table from you and trusted Jesus Christ to be my Savior. I thought that was why you were here."

Not only was I there, right then, at God's command, but I was there, right then, as God's flow through vessel. As tears welled up in my eyes, I said, "I am so sorry that I didn't remember your birthday, but God did! And He sent me here today to tell you Happy Birthday!

"Pam, God loves you! I love you. Come back. We want you to come back."

She said, "Maybe I will. Things haven't been the way I expected them to be since that day, but I can tell you this: The sky is more blue and the leaves more colorful since I entrusted my life to Christ."

Pam did come back. She's still back. She's grown into a beautiful, godly, flow through vessel, and that's what this book is here to help you do, too.

Life with God is not always easy or comprehensible. It's rarely predictable and seldom boring. As we journey forward, I'll introduce you to some flow through analogies and then some examples of how living the flow through life works. After that, I'll explain the exact details to get you connected with God so He can flow through you. You'll also discover some habit-formation strategies to help you move toward habit mastery as a flow through vessel and to do it as quickly as possible.

Welcome to your ultimate existence as a master flow through vessel for God!

Marnie Swedberg

Chapter 2
Foundation-Building Analogies

I love analogies almost as much as I love being God's flow through vessel. I'm a visual learner, so familiar examples help clarify concepts for me.

Below you'll find several flow through analogies, each with its own unique angle as it serves to whet your whistle, prime your pump, and prepare your heart for the best life possible, as a flow through vessel for God.

Let's refresh with the definition of a flow through vessel:

A flow through vessel is any
non-resistant conduit
willing to transmit a substance
from one location, form, or usefulness to another,
for its intended application.

The two main types are Direct Flow Throughs (DFTs), which transport substances, without change, from one location to another, and Metamorphic Flow Throughs (MFTs), which deliver the original substance only after a change to either its form or usefulness.

I love the concept of metamorphosis. An ugly caterpillar enters the safety of a cocoon or pupa and emerges transformed into a moth or butterfly. The cocoon serves as the flow through vessel, facilitating the massive change. An ugly earth crawler emerges as a beautiful fluttering flier.

You are created to serve as a cocoon for supernatural transformation as God flows Himself from heaven to earth through you to others. Like the tiny pupa, you can be a safe place for people going through tough times. Cocooned in God yourself, you can learn to release old habits for better new ones. Both ways, your own life is filled to overflowing with His glory, goodness, and grace—enough for your needs with extra to share.

Direct Flow Through Vessels (DFTs)

Tubes

Did you know that your body boasts over 60,000 miles of arteries, veins, and capillaries? In addition, there are tubes for air, mother's milk, and a fallopian tube to carry eggs from the ovary to the uterus, to create new life.

You have also been gifted with immense spiritual capacity as a flow through vessel for God's love. Your calling includes being all sorts of tube-types, flowing multiple kinds and varieties of blessing from heaven to earth, through your spiritual being, as needed, for His glory.

Consider how an oxygen tube transports fresh, clean air from a purified tank to a weakened individual. All is well as long as the tube is connected, free of debris, and available. But, should the tube ever be disconnected from the tank, get a kink, or become

contaminated in any
way, it can deliver death
instead of life.

**Faking godliness
is ludicrous and
deadly.**

You are surrounded
by weak and wounded
warriors on every side. Dependent on your own resources and
responses, you quickly run out of fresh air for yourself or to share.

Spiritually speaking, it is vital for you to get and stay connected to God. Imagine trying to "fake" oxygen production in an
emergency. Faking godliness is even more ludicrous and deadly.
It doesn't take long for you and everyone around you to start
feeling deprived. Feelings of desperation set in, and you all start
gasping and clawing for air, leading to stress and trauma.

So many people try to act like God, but that's futile. Tapping
into God is totally different from pretending to be God. You are
supposed to be His flow through tube, not a god in your own
right. As you depend on Him for everything, you'll be able to
remain undisturbed by the cares of this world and available to
His input and flow through instructions no matter what's going
on around you.

Hoses

Hoses are bigger than tubes, but also come in a wide variety
of sizes and usages. For example, both garden and fire hoses
channel H_2O. A fire hose delivers so much high-pressured water
that it requires strong arms to keep it under control while a garden hose can be managed by a child.

At times God will flow through your life so violently you'll
feel out of control. Not to worry! *As long as God is in control of
you*, all is well. In fact, that's the plan.

One funny analogy in the Bible teaches us to be "intoxicated"
with God. Like a drunkard staggering around, out of control,

we are to be so receptive to God that He can flow through us without our interference, even if it means we look a little foolish from time to time.

Go with the flow—God's flow.

Go with the flow—God's flow. Whether it's to water spiritual gardens or put out spiritually destructive fires, it's all in a day's work.

As with all DFTs, the size of the passageway is a critical factor. If shrunk, stretched, bent, or blocked, the flow is affected and the ideal results jeopardized. At times like these, we experience and extend to others unnecessary pain instead of spiritual gain.

The goal is to let God flow through us at the velocity of His choice.

Pipes

The largest flow throughs are constructed to carry water, oil, milk, or other substances in quantity. The goal is to get the liquid to where it's supposed to be, at the right time and temperature, and in the purest form possible. It all matters.

When our spiritual pipes have loose fittings, blockages, or get compromised even a little, we can cause unnecessary damage, like the 2010 oil spill in the Gulf of Mexico. Valve failure caused the worst spill of its kind in U.S. history, claiming 11 lives and dumping three million barrels of oil into the Gulf during the 87 days before they capped it off.

When you allow sin in your life, and for as long as you hide it, try harder to fix it, or simply tolerate it, it contaminates God's flow through your life. Your choices are always affecting others, so the goal is to keep your life free of sin, so God's goodness can freely flow through intact, at just the right pace and power level.

Marnie Swedberg

Straws

Not the smallest, but possibly the most fun flow through vessels, I love drinking through straws so long as the liquid in the glass tastes good. A straw doesn't pick and choose what it channels; whatever liquid is in the source container is going to flow directly upward into the mouth of the person sucking on the straw.

When I'm correctly connected with God, I can be sure I'm delivering the exact spiritual refreshment needed. Without God, I'm like a straw stuck in an empty glass: I'm full of hot air and ready to share. Yikes! Look out!

We've got to get and stay connected to God as our Source. Tapped into His love, we have real value to offer others.

Electrical Conduits

My grandpa on my mom's side was an electrician by trade. Mom tells the story of a rare instance when, as a child, she got to go along on a job. Grandpa set her on a chair to one side and then proceeded to fix the broken wiring. At one point, he took charge of the electrical currents and, for her entertainment, sent energy balls flying across the room away from where she sat.

Knowing how to control electrical currents to that degree is why Grandpa was called a master electrician.

I remember my father trying to be like Grandpa, installing the wiring in my new basement bedroom. One night, with a finger still wet from my shower, I flipped the switch, triggering an electrical reaction. I got a pretty good jolt, and it fried the outlet cover, but otherwise it was an innocent mistake.

The analogy is clear: If not properly connected to God, the Ultimate Master Electrician, we can unintentionally deliver painful jolts to those we love. One of the most difficult truths to own is that any good deed, done without God's directive and energy, is vacant of Him and His direction, leaving us full of ourselves. This is less than ideal.

Unfortunately, poor electrical work can even kill. Shawn Hillary shares the story of how her daughter, Anna, was electrocuted due to poor wiring. She was killed while taking a bath even though no hairdryer or other electrical appliance fell into the tub. Instead, a deadly dose of current made its way through the hot and cold water taps, delivering enough voltage into the tub to kill her.

The entire story is an analogy, but the part I want to focus on here is that the family experienced tingly sensations when turning on the faucets from the day they moved in; they just didn't perceive those indicators as a threat.

In the same way, negative vibes, unpleasant surprises, or jolts of life-sapping energy flow from self-generated responses—alone or mixed in with God's. I see this in my own life when my dependence on God digresses into personal dependence.

> The last thing God intends is for His children to hurt others with His power.

If I fail to take corrective action, based on God's gentle nudging in my heart or the subtle reactions of those around me, it's a quick trip from being an energizer to an electrifier, and nobody wants to get electrocuted!

The last thing God intends is for His children to hurt others with His power. Yet, I venture to guess you have personally experienced at least one killer conversation where a self-proclaimed God-lover zapped you, leaving you shocked, stunned, or eager to avoid further contact with them or God.

This is the result of a faulty connection or excessive charge. It happens when a God-lover adds "self" to what God is flowing through her. She becomes lethal.

Marnie Swedberg

Get connected to God and stay consciously aware of your dependence on Him. If you notice even the slightest hint of feedback from someone, like Anna's family feeling "tingles," take immediate corrective action by unplugging "self" and reconnecting consciously with God.

We've looked at a few direct flow through analogies, but we've only scratched the surface. They can be found everywhere. Like the elevator analogy, we get to go up or down, with or without God; it's always a choice.

Metamorphic Flow Throughs (MFTs)

The electrical analogy from above is an example of both direct and metamorphic flow throughs. Electrical wires carry voltage from source to outlet, where the type of outlet determines the output.

Electricity is very versatile. My grandpa could connect it to power a whole building or to throw lightning balls across the room. While traveling to other countries, we rely on adapters to convert energy as needed to accomplish our daily routines. The ability to increase or decrease amperage and control the feed works only as well as the conductors, connections, conduits, and breaker switches involved.

Sin in our lives can cause us to deliver 1000 amps to someone when 100 would suffice. Again, we need to look to Jesus as our power source and stay focused on Him. Jesus both feeds our lives with supernatural energy and modulates its release for His glory.

Corrective Lenses

Seeing out of focus was the story of my life during my first three decades, so one of my favorite MFTs is corrective lenses. I wore thick glasses to see clearly prior to my Lasik surgery in

2000, when my sister, Vicki, and I underwent the procedure on consecutive days.

At the pre-op exam, we asked for our "numbers" because we'd been collecting counts from friends before our arrival. People with perfect vision boasted 20/20, the standard measure of what can be seen at 20 feet, while those wearing thick glasses ranged up to 20/400.

We knew our eyes were bad off, and I not only had poor vision, but also astigmatism. I couldn't even wear contact lenses, because every time I blinked, my eyes flipped the contacts around, causing blurry vision for several post-blink seconds. Vicki's eyes were just as bad.

We were dying for the official verdict, but when we pressed the nurse for the number, she said we were "count finger." Dissatisfied, we asked her again for a number.

She said, "Your eyes don't have a number. We just hold up our hand and hope you can see how many fingers."

Going from that level of dependence on a pair of glasses to 20/20 vision the next day was mind bending. It took me over three years before I totally stopped reaching for my glasses in the morning. I'd push up the air on my nose where my glasses used to sit. I'd walk into a warm building on a cold day and reach up to remove the fogged over lenses, only to find they were no longer there.

Habits are an amazing thing, and eyeglasses are a perfect example of a metamorphic flow through vessel. They correct nearsightedness by diverging light before it hits the retina so it can be converged by the cornea to produce an accurate image.

Glasses change our perception without changing the environment. Without God's intervention, we all face spiritual nearsightedness and misread what we are experiencing; life is blurry or incomprehensible.

Marnie Swedberg

To enjoy abundant life, put on the corrective lenses God provides. Hold everything up to the truth revealed in the Bible. Not only will this create more peace and joy in your own life, but you'll be able to share that perspective with those around you.

Human Body

There are probably dozens of flow through analogies to be found inside the human body. Let's look here at some of your body's systems, each with its own point to make:

- The muscular system grows by flexing as we lift ever heavier weights. Our faith muscles grow as we lift heavier prayer burdens to Jesus.
- The immune system defends against disease. The spiritual immune system defends against dis-ease.
- The nervous system controls everything. Our spiritual nerves send, receive, and process spiritual impulses from major to minor, like the subtle clues we discussed above.
- The respiratory system enables us to breathe air. Spiritually, we need to breathe the air of prayer.
- The digestive system breaks down everything we take in, either eliminating it as a toxin or utilizing it for health. Spiritually, we digest every emotion, attitude, and visual we take in. Doing so with God allows us to process these in a way that avoids spiritual indigestion.

The list goes on, and within each system we find additional analogies. In the digestive system, for example, we find the elimination

Glasses change our perception without changing the environment.

process, God's built-in design for separating the good from the bad and then carrying waste and toxins safely out of the body. Spiritual toxins are eliminated in like manner.

Garbage In, Garbage Out

Just as the body eliminates waste, all of us have trash bins full of rubbish that need to be removed from our surroundings each week.

Have you ever marveled at the existence of garbage men? I cannot fathom getting up every morning to go collect garbage, so I am grateful to God for these guys. We love our garbage men. I still leave them treats every now and again, and my kids were a great help with this effort when they were young. In fact, my son, Timothy, made friends with garbage man, Tim, and one Christmas the crew stood at our front door, extending a wrapped gift to my little boy.

God uses everything!

Do you realize that even a dump truck is God's analogy to help you understand how to be a flow through vessel for His glory? God uses everything!

Garbage in, garbage out. But it's not a direct flow through because the trash gets crushed before it's expelled at the dump.

Next time someone dumps on you, pick up the trash and put it in God's trash truck. Give it all to Him. Watch Him drive the junk away from your life, crushing the nasty yuck as it goes.

Honestly, God is the best trash master ever.

This is where we can get it mucked up. We behave like the trash or the truck instead of like the trash man. Don't do that! Don't squish all that trash down inside you, or throw it around as if no one cares. Be the trash man: Hand all the trash you're given directly to Jesus and let Him smash it to smithereens.

Then wave with gratitude as He drives it away from your life in His big trash truck.

Plants

Before His death and resurrection, Jesus gave his disciples the flow through analogy of a vine: Jesus is the vine, God is the vine dresser, and we are the branches. He explained how we need to stay connected to the vine to bear good fruit.

Being a fruit bearer can be misunderstood as referring to personal responsibility instead of positional dependence. We tend to believe we are to somehow produce the fruit of godly love,

Our job is simply to be fruit holders—fruit bearers vs. fruit producers.

joy, peace, patience, kindness, goodness, gentleness, faithfulness, and self-control. But that's impossible. Instead, God's plan is for Him to produce His fruit through us. Our job is simply to be fruit holders—fruit bearers vs. fruit producers.

This is so important: Being a fruit bearer should not be misunderstood as referring to personal responsibility but as positional dependence.

Imagine a dead branch lying on your lawn: It's lost its connection to the tree, to its source of life, and can no longer bear fruit. It's dead or dying.

In a similar way, we are not capable of bearing God's fruit without God flowing it to and through us. As long as we perceive ourselves as fruit producers, instead of fruit hangers (fruit bearers), we'll keep trying and trying to produce the godly fruit of love, peace, kindness, and more, and we'll keep failing.

Any fruit we produce without God is not God's fruit; it's our counterfeit fruit. It is our attempt at doing godly life without

God. It's fraud, and besides that, it's not very satisfying for us or anyone around us.

When we embrace the truth of what Jesus called us to be, fruit bearers, we can relax into the process and enjoy all four seasons, however fast they come around.

- In the summer, our tree is full of fruit, being consumed by all who hunger.
- In the fall, our leaves turn beautiful colors and provide visual joy to all who see us.
- In the winter, all is calm. No fruit and no worries. 'T is the season to rest.
- In the spring, we burst into beautiful blooms, with the promise of fresh fruit right around the corner.

Understanding God's ways changes everything. Patience with His process provides peace. Confidence in His plan brings joy.

New Life

The cycles of birth, life, and death are interwoven into every living thing. A seed must die to allow a plant to live, and a human seed must be planted in order for new life to exist.

Whenever we encounter an opportunity or a God-seed, we experience blessing. For example, I have three beautiful adult children—three amazing blessings from God. My sister, Marla, has four babies in heaven and two daughters here on earth. All six children are blessings from God: Two for now, four for later.

Sometimes bearing fruit is painful, like the labor and delivery of a baby. Other times it's snuffed out with results opposite of our hopes and dreams, like Marla's miscarriages and still birth. More often, it involves a long, confusing process from seed to full bloom. Whichever the case, the wait will be worth it.

Marnie Swedberg

Let's identify some of the options we have as a flow through vessel when being offered a new seed from God:

- No flow. Ignore or reject the seed as impossible or impractical. Unfortunately, I think this is probably the fate of most of God's invitations to us.

God is the
Master Gardener.

- Temporary flow. Plant the seed by faith, but then uproot it with our doubts.
- Restored flow. Recognize we've uprooted a seed and replant it immediately with prayer, praising God for another chance.
- Hampered flow. Plant and water the seedling in a greenhouse environment, tenderly caring for it as it grows. This is ideal unless we come to believe we are responsible for the plants' protection, and we refuse to move it from the greenhouse to the freedom of a garden when it's ready. This choice can stunt its growth or kill the plant, neither of which are God's plan.
- God's flow. Allow God to apply His love and provision to every seed we plant at every stage of development, watching it grow without taking responsibility for its growth.

God is the Master Gardener. Our role is to depend on Him and rest in His ability to flow through us and others as He deems best. Herein lies the joy of life.

I believe any option other than the last one feels to God like a miscarriage feels to a woman. It breaks His heart because He had good plans for a good outcome.

Sometimes life is just plain confusing—whether a human child or an idea seed is killed early, we face an unmet expectation and experience the death of a dream. It can be utterly perplexing.

I've often asked God, "Why do you plant a seed of hope and then not allow it to come to fruition?"

I don't have the answer yet, but I do know God is not vindictive at all. He is not allowing these things to torture us! In fact, I have come to realize that God is compassionate and cares tenderly whenever we experience this type of loss. He is personally familiar with exactly how we feel, because He experiences deep sadness every time anyone ignores, rejects, or mocks His invitation for intimacy.

Forgiveness

God extends forgiveness to us for hurting Him no matter what we do, what we've ever done, or what we will do in the future to cause Him pain. We, on the other hand, are not so fast to "forgive" God when He allows us to be disappointed.

It isn't exactly forgiveness we need to extend to God when He allows a dream to be crushed or a loss to occur. But we accuse Him of all sorts of bad intentions. If He were a human, we'd say we needed to forgive Him and move on.

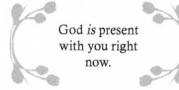
God *is* present with you right now.

It hurts us when God doesn't come through for us the way we want. We often feel He could have or should have intervened and that He's guilty of something, even if we aren't fully able to verbalize what we're holding against Him.

As long as we carry this misplaced angst (or unforgiveness) toward God, we jeopardize intimacy and prevent His life from flowing through us.

What's lacking is faith. As it relates to God, He requires us to believe He exists and rewards everyone who seeks Him. This faith comes only after we lay down our anger, and in moments of disillusionment, this can be hard to do.

A roller coaster analogy is perfect here: You would be crazy to get on a roller coaster if you weren't convinced it was safe to do so. It would be suicide.

Forgiveness asks you to put all your faith and trust in God as you extend the unthinkable to the unlovable. You'd be crazy to offer forgiveness to God or others who you feel have deeply wounded you, unless you know God is good and has your best interests at heart.

Jesus modeled amazing forgiveness for us from the cross as He looked down and saw the men who were torturing Him and putting Him to death. In a moment of ultimate faith, He said, "Father, forgive them. They know not what they do."

The soldiers may not have realized He was God-in-flesh, but they knew full well they were killing Him. They knew it hurt Him terribly, yet He trusted God and forgave them.

We are to extend this degree of forgiveness to everyone we meet and the only way is to let God flow it through us. That can only happen when we trust God and release any sense of angst toward Him.

God Is Incomprehensible Yet Fully Involved

I have a blind friend, Janet Perez Eckles, who recently returned from South America where she had traveled to several speaking engagements. She told me that she experiences little difference between being with God or a human travel companion, since she can see neither. Both are present with her by faith, not sight. She prefers to travel the world "alone" with God.

Try this: Shut your eyes right now and realize that God is with you.

Janet can't see, so maybe it's easier for her to believe God is present with her. Your "handicap" of good vision may require you to apply extra faith, but it's worth the effort!

God *is* present with you right now. He is fully good, fully God, and fully available to you in the most personal and practical ways imaginable. But God is not manageable. Don't try to manage God.

Throughout this book I use phrases like "get connected to God," "let God," "allow God," or "get God." I want to clarify what I do and don't mean.

- God is not a puppet: You cannot "get God" or "make God" do anything, unless God delights in it. Rest in who He is and who He created you to be.
- Do trust God without trying to train Him to see things your way. He's the God. You're the vessel.
- Don't worry about taking advantage of God. It's not possible. You will never "pull one over" on God or "get away with" anything at His expense.

And don't try to "force" God onto others.

You are not supposed to be a convicter, convincer, or a conductor. You are created to be a conduit. Rest in the reality that a flow through vessel is only responsible to stay connected and available. When someone ignores God, you, or the offer of spiritual refreshment flowing through you, don't take it personally. Just relax with God and remain available to Him. There's so much peace here, and you need not worry about running out of resources.

As you nurture your dependence on God, you will always have enough for your every need, with plenty to spare, and extra to share.

Marnie Swedberg

My friend from India, Nishma, experiences God's provision through what she calls, "the drawer." Poor, sick, blind, and needy people flow in and out of her ministry daily seeking funds for medicine, water, and more. Nishma prays with them, opens "the drawer," and gives them whatever funds she finds inside, sometimes none.

When pressed for details about how money gets into the drawer, she looks dumbfounded, as if the question is a joke. It is obvious to her that God, her supplier, fills the drawer as needed, just as God, Janet's favorite travel companion, shows her where to go and what to do.

Janet fully expects God to lead her where He knows she should go. Nishma expects God to provide for legitimate needs while displaying an empty drawer to people seeking funds for godless intent.

The beauty is that their God, my God, the God of the universe, longs to be your God, too. He created you in order for you to have a close, personal, flow through relationship with Him. He knows what you need, when you need it, and is in the perfect position to supply it to and through you.

Chapter 3
Real-Life Stories to Develop the Dream

Worrying, trying harder, and always feeling like you are falling short is the opposite of God's will for your life. News flash: Your self-effort is not impressing God. Remember, to impress God, you'd need to be better than Him at something. Impossible!

The 4R Response

I nearly named this book "The 4R Response," which is my description of what comes second nature to mature Christians (those God-lovers you know who are truly good, loving, and kind people). Each has stopped trying to impress God and has adopted a life of practical faith. They trust God's willingness and ability to flow Himself through them, and He does.

We'll expand on these later, but here I want to introduce the most powerful prayer pattern I know for times of crisis, crushing words, or confusing circumstances. The 4R's are:

> **Recognize** you need help and that God wants to help by flowing His response to and through you.
>
> **Release** your pain, problem, mental processes, or predicament to Him.
>
> **Receive** His choice of exchange gifts for you (often peace, hope, faith, or comfort).
>
> **Respond** with a "Thank You" and a willingness to assist.

Every person who has mastered the habit of letting God flow through has a similar process going on consciously or subconsciously.

If you miss even one of the Rs, you may spin your spiritual wheels, continuing to try harder for lack of knowing something better to do. The 4R Response, in whatever rendition you choose to apply it, is what I use and have taught for years as an easy way to stay in the flow of God's love all the time.

Whenever we experience pain of any kind, something inside us cries out for God. Have you ever wondered why?

Habits & Addictions

Emotional trauma of any kind creates a vacuum in our souls. When we grasp for anything other than God to satisfy the uncomfortable feelings of emptiness it creates, we give power to the vacuum, and this can lead to bad habits, addictions, and self-perpetuated alienation from God.

The bottom line is that we experience only what we are aware of and tapped into at any given moment. If we remain consciously sensitive to God's presence, drinking from His well, we enjoy His life flowing through us. If not, whatever we've replaced Him with will dictate our experience.

I know because I've done it both ways. I still do it both ways.

It's insane to think a cigarette or a chunk of chocolate will make us feel better after an intense or stressful encounter, but we all have our own go-to responses. We want something, anything, to override our bad feelings, and we want that something to be tangible.

God created us to need Him in the same way we need air.

God is invisible.

God created us to need Him in the same way we need air. Any perversion of that plan leads to spiritual suffocation. This is as true for the person who has not yet met God as it is for the God-lover who doesn't understand how to let Him flow through. The first hasn't gotten hooked up yet, while the second is already connected through Jesus, but has allowed something to interfere with God's flow.

If anything other than God has been flowing through your life, let's change that right now by creating the habit of embracing God as your one and only Source.

It will take time and awareness to develop this new habit because, similar to our need for oxygen, we are usually oblivious to our total dependence on it until something goes wrong. All of a sudden, we begin to suffocate, and the gasping begins. We claw at the air for anything that appears to be a reasonable alternative for the original source of life.

We see this all the time. In a crisis, people either say a prayer, spew a string of swear words, or reach for a God-replacement like a drink, drag, or donut.

Whatever you do when you are in pain, that is your personal go-to. While gasping for spiritual air, you grasp that substitute instead of reaching for God. But just as an asthmatic learns to instinctively reach for his inhaler whenever his airflow is threatened, you can create a new habit.

You can learn to reach for God as your first and automatic response in any crisis, large or small. My goal in this book is to help you understand how to transfer your allegiance to the most powerful go-to of all time: God. It is even possible to relate to God when you can't think clearly.

If you show me a beautiful person who's fully dependent on God, I'll bet they've lived a life full of trials and traumas, choosing God and choosing joy along the way. Their troubles, like fire refining gold, have allowed them to mature to a high level of dependence on God—and it is His beauty we see flowing through their yielded lives. They are "master flow through vessels."

Meet Some Master Flow Through Vessels

Before we dive into the how-tos of becoming a master flow through vessel, I want to share some stories of people I know and love who've modeled this lifestyle through life's toughest challenges. They've trusted God, one faith-choice at a time, and their stories are as motivational as they are inspirational.

Marie

The shrill sound of the ambulance siren drove the throbbing inside her head to a new level of agony. She was vomiting every few minutes and the pain was relentless, like a vice grip ever tightening around her brain.

Spinning, spiking, nauseating lightning bolts of pain were all she knew. But during her few lucid thoughts, she was experiencing something almost worse: intense hopelessness.

Julie

After the shock, horror, and disbelief overwhelmed her mind like a plastic bag covering her face, she went into instant denial: He couldn't be gay! This couldn't be happening to them!

Her mind whirled in a dizzying dance with despair. She'd believed him. She had even defended his absences. Who would come to her rescue now? If someone came, what could they do?

There was no one to call, nowhere to turn, and nowhere to hide. Her entire life was disintegrating before her very eyes as she crumpled to the floor, curled into a fetal position, and sobbed as disillusionment and fear gripped her soul.

Tom

He was alive. That's all he knew. His body lay dead still, tubes and machines the only things supporting his failing functions—at least for the moment.

He couldn't move, so he had to just stay and lay; wait and see. The fear he felt was like a ferocious fire. While doctors could potentially treat his body, he was utterly alone on that bed, except for the gnawing, persistent presence of fear.

Cheryl

It had been a long and exhausting labor followed by a painful delivery. She'd actually screamed in horror when they held up her deformed child.

Now her entire body was shaking violently, going into shock, even as her confused mind was hyperventilating between motherly instincts and alarm at what she had just seen.

Laura

As she cried her way through the confession she'd prayerfully drafted, the only thing she could see were his eyes—hurt, betrayed, swelling with tears, and worst of all, hardening with every word she spoke.

She had known she had to confess, and that it would be hard, but she'd fasted and prayed. She'd worded things as carefully as she could to protect his heart. And she had believed—with her whole heart, she'd believed God would honor her honesty by helping him forgive her.

But that was not happening. Instead, she was watching his heart break with every new syllable. Her confusion and sadness were paralleled only by her sense of God's betrayal. She wondered if this was His cruel way of punishing her for her original failure.

She sat glued to the scene of her husband's broken-heartedness, wanting to salvage something—anything. She felt a frantic need to comfort him, but all she could find inside was emptiness.

~ ~ ~

Have you ever been able to relate to Marie? In so much pain—hopeful, yet hopeless, because the relief that was coming wouldn't be enough, or couldn't last for long?

> *Hopelessness seeps into the soul like the*
> *claws of a tiger into its prey.*

How about Julie? Have you ever feared that everything you believed in, everything you'd done up until that point, everything you knew, was gone?

> *Escape or suicidal thoughts come rushing in like a tsunami,*
> *wiping away every hopeful idea in their path.*

Marnie Swedberg

Tom's fear and helplessness may be more akin to the time you lost a child in a crowded mall, or sat near the bedside of a loved one whose life hung by a thread.

> *Being helplessly dependent can be a lonely*
> *and terrifying place.*

Or, when was the last time you went into physical or mental hyperventilation, like Cheryl, after receiving astoundingly bad news?

> *Shock is the body's defense system when the input*
> *we are receiving would otherwise blow our brains.*

Laura had made a wrong choice, followed by a right choice. She had done the best thing she could, in the most loving way she knew how, and it had backfired.

> *Have you ever felt that God betrayed you*
> *in your most vulnerable moment?*

~ ~ ~

Marie was a master flow through vessel. She used every lucid moment, as the ambulance sped along, to mentally grasp the most powerful word in the human language, "Jesus."

As Julie sobbed uncontrollably over the choices her husband had made, the only thing she knew to do was to exchange every erupting thought for just One: the name of Jesus.

Each time the arrows of fear stabbed at Tom's heart, he silently raised his only defense heavenward, "Jesus!"

> Exchange every
> erupting thought for just
> One: the name of Jesus.

Between gasps for air, Cheryl automatically kicked into a habit she'd developed during her other difficult labors: Breathe in: "Jesus!" Puff out: air. Breathe in: "Jesus!" Puff out: air.

Baffled beyond belief, Laura didn't know how to respectfully do it, but she knew she had to reach out for God, so she kicked into her newly formed mode of operandi: Choosing Jesus. Despite the fact that her attitude felt disrespectful to her, she honored God by throwing her pain His way, mentally screaming out, "Jesus! Jesus! Jesus!"

~ ~ ~

Unless Marie had been in the habit of calling on Jesus in times of trauma, her only response to her pain would have been to endure it the best she could.

She could have been all alone with the
hopelessness in her head as she died.
Instead, she experienced the presence of God as
He prepared to take her home that day.

But for the fact that Julie had been practicing breathing Jesus for years, she may never have gotten up off that floor. Instead, not only did she get up, but she also got busy forgiving her way-ward husband.

They are still married, happy, and healthy. She says her life is
better than it ever could have been before the truth came out.

Since his diagnosis in his youth, Tom could have hated God for his health issues, but instead developed a "hospital habit" that served him well for years. He says, "The place I feel most at peace is when I am lying on a hospital bed, completely out of control."

Marnie Swedberg

Whenever his health scares him, he breathes the
air of prayer and finds God there, ready to calm,
comfort, and heal him, in His way and time.

After walking through seemingly sleepless decades, including surgeries, therapies, extended hospital stays, and financial trauma beyond belief, Cheryl and her family are still tapping into God every single day.

Breathing Jesus is a way of life for Cheryl and
she radiates health, hope, and happiness.

Laura's marriage was salvaged, but her husband's wounds have not yet fully healed. She, on the other hand, is a loving wife who trusts and obeys her way through each new emotional high and low, finding hope and joy in Jesus.

She is still believing for her marriage miracle.

In the meantime, she is loved and forgiven by
Jesus Christ, her eternal Bridegroom.

Section II

How-Tos

Chapter 4
Hang On for the
Ride of Your Life

*L*ife as God's flow through vessel may be best compared to a roller coaster ride. God flows through us, but we are also flowing through Him. He is in us and we are fully secure in Him.

A roller coaster is the flow through vessel for times when you just want to have fun! You fly high and go fast, get dumped upside down, and feel motion-induced sensations, all the while knowing you'll be able to get off the ride in pretty much the same shape as when you got on. Sure, there may be moments you hate being out of control, and you may at times wish the ride would stop, but you know it's OK, it's just a ride.

Remove the confidence in the safety of the ride and you would be crazy to get on. The ride would be sheer terror and lunacy, and would definitely result in your injury or death.

In Section V we'll address any "trust issues" you may have with God, but here I want to take a few minutes and use the roller coaster analogy to help you understand how to trust God through a life riveted with terrifying highs, lows, and blind corners.

The ride of your life with God looks something like this:

Buckle up. The spiritual equivalent of climbing aboard and buckling up is trusting Jesus Christ to be Lord of your life. It is giving Him complete control as you take the passenger seat. This transaction guarantees His companionship and protection along the way as well as your safe arrival to your final destination, heaven.

Ready. Set. Go. You take a deep breath and feel anticipation co-mingled with fear. You are entering the great unknown and as you exit the station, your faith is full. You feel confident you can handle anything life can throw at you. You are safe in God's care, and you remind yourself that it's only a ride. Heaven is your home.

Steep climb. Your brain and body know something must be coming, but you are not quite sure what, so tension rises as you near the summit. Spiritually, this fear can either drive you to Jesus as you climb toward the peak, or it can crush you with terror as you watch all your familiar control mechanisms fall away. You choose faith over fear.

Choose faith over fear.

High above it all. Precariously perched atop the world, you have zero control and are utterly dependent on God for everything. If you spent your ride up talking with God, your arrival will be a spiritual high. However, if you let your mind worry, you'll find yourself frozen with fear here. Being out of control is one of the most terrifying feelings a human can face. Knowing God is in control is its exact opposite—peace that passes all understanding.

Free fall. With much less force pushing on your body parts, you feel weightless even while experiencing a sinking feeling. A free fall can be triggered by a disappointment or unmet expectation. If you were consciously aware of God's presence just prior to the fall, the trip down can be full of joy despite the plunge off the peak. Replacing fear with freshly fueled faith makes you aware that God Himself is carrying you and any sinking sensation is easily overcome by that reality.

Around a blind corner. Shocking life experiences force you to face your faith, or lack of it: Are you trusting God or your own resources to get you around this bend? Press your life into each intense turn of events with God and you'll experience some serious spiritual growth. There are few things more exciting than seeing personal progress in life, and rapid growth is available to you especially during times that require intense faith. Focus here on exercising your faith muscles.

Speed. Did you know the body can't determine velocity, only changes in speed? A blind person experiences the ride in a completely different way without the visuals zipping past, alerting them of increased speed. When terrified by what you see happening in your life, shut your spiritual eyes and pray. This is what's meant by "blind faith." At times like these, remind yourself to look up more than you look around. Keep your eyes on Jesus!

Upside-down. Your brain is spinning to translate its status into something comprehensible. You are in the air, rushing through space, with no visible support systems. Knowing God is in charge of the ride makes all the difference between hopelessness and delight, allowing you to soar through circumstances that would otherwise leave you traumatized.

Up again. This time you face additional internal stress because your brain is fully aware of what might come next. Whether you are being rushed to the hospital again, facing a second court hearing on the same charges, or going to the dentist, the second time around is often harder than the first. Choose to connect with God meaningfully on the way toward the dreaded event to find yourself filled to overflowing with His joy as you prepare for the required descent. Just trust God!

Just trust God!

Air time. As you drop downward, the g-force crushes you while each part of your body accelerates individually. Nothing is where it's supposed to be. Free falls are spiritually exhilarating while emotionally exhausting all at once. Do you know anyone who has paid to go bungee jumping, just for fun? They might not be able to verbalize this, but their enjoyment of the fall was equal to the degree they trusted the operator. When you feel afraid, check in with your Operator. And if you fail to pray your way to the peak, cry out to Jesus on your way down. Smile as you remind God how much you love His super talent of swooping in and rescuing you from your runaway emotions.

Inside a dark tunnel. The random lights and cold air rushing past are intended to create drama and build anticipation; it works. If you are confidently trusting God, this part of the ride is a wonderful reprieve from life's chaos. Shut your eyes. Hear the rattle of the car clicking along the track. Feel the blast of cool air as you say a prayer and recognize God is there. Enjoy this part of life's ride with curiosity. There are only two choices: anxiety or curiosity. The latter is faith's way of freeing God to provide the best possible outcomes, while the former quenches His creative juices from flowing through you. Your body is buckled in, but your brain has to make choices.

> You will learn to love your loopy life.

A loop-the-loop. Your body is driven straight forward as the track takes your car upside down, pushing you off the floor while the inertia glues you to it. You get a false sense of gravity, which feels frightening, even though this is one of the safest parts of the ride. Full dependence on God gives Him the opportunity to flow jaw-dropping, loop-the-loops through your life. It feels precarious to be out of personal control and in God's, but it's the safest place in the world. You will learn to love your loopy life.

Coming out of the loop. You feel heavy and your heart is pounding fast because every cell in your body has just been shaken out of position again. It is 100% normal to experience an emotional low after a spiritual high. One Bible prophet even asked God to kill him after a mountain top experience. As always, run every emotion to Jesus so He can provide perspective, peace, hope, and help. In the case of the depressed prophet, God sent food, water, and sleep—a prescription you'll become accustomed to following many of life's extreme events.

The rest of the ride. As life thrusts you through these gyrations repeatedly in random, unexpected progressions, God carries you all the way. Learn to expect the unexpected and go with the flow, fully trusting Him. God wants to take care of everything that concerns you both here and in eternity.

The ride slows to a stop. I'm curious now: What do you expect when you get off the ride of your life? Maybe heaven? That's exactly what God promises to you once you've chosen to get on the ride of your life with Him.

Life with God is exciting! It's got its highs, its humor, and its humbling lows.

Just this morning, on the day I am writing this part of the book, I became an Amazon #1 Best Selling Author for the first time ever. After 19 years and 12 books, one finally made me a best selling author. What a thrill!

What happened next is real life. I heard a noise in the kitchen and walked out to find the dog busy going through the trash she'd spread all over the floor.

I just laughed out loud with God as I started cleaning up the mess He knew could humble my quickly soaring pride.

Life is full of highs, lows, and reality checks. C'est la vie.

Once you buckle in with God, prepare for the ride of your life. Whether or not you enjoy roller coasters, nothing can quite prepare you for the supernatural highs, miraculous moments, or twists and turns of a life yielded to God as His flow through vessel.

Dangling In Thin Air

Almost all day, everyday, you can experience a joy-filled life with Jesus: exhilarating, full of surprising delights, and sometimes frightening due to scary circumstances, coupled with a goldy perspective.

Trusting God in no way means you escape life on earth. Practically every time the Bible records an angel appearing to a human, they say the same thing, "Do not fear," or "Be not afraid."

Life can be terrifying. Trusting God makes life worth living as He delivers sanity to drama and hope to trauma. Doing life as God's flow through vessel means you have instant and ongoing access to His love, power, peace, and provision. His availability to you means you need never do anything by yourself again.

I asked my nephew, 12-year-old Trey, to recount for you his third roller coaster ride, which he went on alone since no one in our group wanted to go again so soon. It was the terrifying ShieKra at Busch Gardens. He'd loved his first two rounds and just had to go again, even alone.

At the first peak, intentionally, the ShieKra pauses for dramatic effect before plunging down. At the top of the second peak, the delay replays. On Trey's ride, it paused so long that everyone aboard realized the ride had broken. There they hung, dangling over the edge, looking 90 feet straight down, knowing they would free fall at any moment, but not knowing when.

In Trey's words, "At first, I thought it was part of the ride, but then I realized we were stuck and I started freaking out. I was shaking and really scared. The three girls near me were screaming."

You've already been here at some point in your life: stuck, emotionally staring straight down at a drop-off, with people screaming at or near you. Life is full of ups and downs.

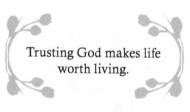

Trusting God makes life worth living.

The sooner you learn to let God flow His peace and joy through you, through it all, the sooner you'll be able to relax and enjoy watching God get you out of every impossible situation.

Trey went on, "After a long time, a lady talked to us over the loudspeaker. She said the ride was broken but they were fixing it." Here he paused to explain, "The lady called to reassure us."

That's exactly what prayer does for you: It brings God's powerful presence into your conscious awareness, comforting your fearful heart.

> Jesus, talk to me about this from Your perspective.

There is a simple prayer I want to teach you for times when you feel afraid or confused. It goes like this, "Jesus, talk to me about this from Your perspective."

God is not surprised or upset by your predicaments. He offers you the opportunity to experience them with Him, at peace.

The lady on the loud speaker was quiet for a time and then, Trey explained, "The next time we heard her voice, she said, 'Prepare for sudden movement.' And right after that, we took the plunge."

God is in the business of preparing you for the future challenges He foresees coming your way. Even if He goes silent for a season, or allows you to feel frightened for a little while, He is faithfully extending grace to you, growing your patience, faith, and trust in Him. And He'll get you through, no matter what.

I asked Trey how that ride compared to other roller coaster rides he's been on since and he said, "It wasn't my scariest."

Intrigued, I inquired as to which ride was scariest. He not only answered, but he gave his reason. He said, "The Falcon's Fury was even scarier; the ShieKra drop wasn't so bad. It was just the waiting."

Isn't that the truth! Climbs and falls can feel scary, but waiting without knowing is one of the hardest things God will ever call you to do. Next time you are facing a frightening wait for news about a family member, your health, a job, or anything else, invite Jesus to stay in the lobby of life with you. He's your best friend. He asks if you'd like Him to go with you to every waiting room experience, shedding light on the fact that He is orchestrating all things for your good.

I asked Trey if there was anything else he thought I should know about his experience. To my surprise, he completed the loop without prompting when he said, "Nothing, except that when it stopped I had a really bad craving for fried chicken!"

Wow! Here it is! This is what we all experience during or after any major trauma. We desperately want God, but we don't recognize our feelings as that. We experience hunger—a craving for something that equals comfort to us. For Trey, it was fried chicken.

When we place our faith and trust in God, He turns every evil plot into something good, every fearful thought into a faithful response, and every confusing situation into a cause for joy. These results sometimes take a while to show up, while at other times they materialize within seconds or minutes of a cry for help.

God longs to be your first and only go-to Source for everything. He has good plans for your life, is

> God longs to be your first and only go-to Source for everything.

bent on your character development, and offers a retirement plan that is literally out of this world.

Jesus is Preparing Heaven for You

If you are still having doubts about trusting God with your life in the here-and-now, I'd be curious to know your thoughts about heaven. I believe that if you think heaven sounds lame, you'll feel conflicted trying to invest your time into a relationship with heaven's God, because it's a two-for-one deal.

I wish I could erase from your mind every image of heaven that includes cherubs on clouds playing harps. Those pictures are ridiculous and may be causing you to doubt God's goodness, realism, or even existence. It's like marketing a Rolls Royce by making a commercial featuring a block of wood with marshmallow wheels. There is simply no comparison and it does injustice to the real thing.

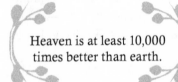

Heaven is at least 10,000 times better than earth.

Heaven is at least 10,000 times better than earth.

God spent just six days creating everything we see from Bora Bora to Banff. Locally, just look at a sunrise or night sky to see His creative handiwork. This God's got talent, and He works super fast!

Before Jesus left for heaven, after His time-changing 33 years on earth, He said He was going back to prepare a place for us. It's been 2000 years. If He worked at it only 1/10th as hard, heaven's layout still beats earth's by thousands to one. Nice digs, I'm thinking!

When God describes heaven for us in the Bible, He intentionally uses words that have meaning to us: streets of gold, gates of pearls, a crystal sea, and so forth.

If I was assigned the task of describing a place beyond comprehension, I think using gold, our most valuable asset, as pavement is brilliant! We can deduce He's trying to tell us that the best is yet to come.

There is a heaven where evil has no place. It is where the desires of our hearts come to fruition. Jesus bought our priceless admission ticket with His death on the cross. On earth, He was the ultimate human flow through vessel for God, and from heaven, through His Spirit, He longs to be our creative, powerful, loving Source.

Jesus, while fully God, was fully man. He was wholly dependent on God for everything and this is what it means to "be like Jesus." God never intended us to just act like Jesus: Acting is acting, and it's a fact that even the best performance cannot precisely match the real deal.

God's plan is for us to trust and depend on Him in the same way Jesus did. When we do, we get to be His personal flow through vessels, just like Jesus was.

Chapter 5
How to Move Beyond Drama, Trauma & Self-Induced Stress

Remember how my friends from Chapter 3 were in so much pain they could barely think? They simply cried out, "Jesus, Jesus, Jesus," over and over, until the pain released enough for them to kick into their own version of a sincere prayer conversation with God about their circumstances.

A great place for you to begin is to practice the "Jesus, Jesus, Jesus" response, over and over and over, until you own it. Memorize it as if it's your spiritual 911. Use it as if you are shooting an arrow at a target: The arrow is the prayer, the target is God's heart. Do not skip this part!

You are like a baby flow through vessel. Babies learn to listen, then babble, then

You are like a baby flow through vessel.

understand, and finally speak. Their first words are gibberish, followed by one word, two words, short sentences, and so on. In the same way, God doesn't expect you to memorize a four-step response before you master His name. Start simple and grow from there. That's how God created you—to develop and grow one step at a time.

Once you've mastered the habit of calling out the name of Jesus when in distress, it's time to move on to the next level of mastery. Internalizing the 4Rs will help you move past drama, trauma, and self-induced stress toward a life of peace, joy, and eternal significance.

Whenever facing a challenge, sadness, setback, pain, or any other big emotion, and immediately after letting the name and person of Jesus calm you enough to think, I encourage you to reach for the 4Rs in rapid succession:

> **Recognize** you're in trouble and God wants to help by flowing through you.
>
> **Release** your pain, problem, mental processes, or predicament to Him.
>
> **Receive** His choice of exchange gifts for you (often peace, hope, faith, or comfort).
>
> **Respond** with a "Thank You" and a willingness to assist.

As soon as you are able, memorize these. Practice, practice, practice. Repeat and internalize them until they become automatic in any crisis. In order to help you learn them, let's go through each in more detail.

1. Recognize you're in trouble and God wants to help by flowing through you.

Most of us have the first part of this "R" down pat: We frequently realize we're in trouble! It's the second part that gets us. We usually don't reach for God. We seem to prefer pastries, pornography, or self-pity, choosing a familiar habit or addiction instead of God. By doing so, we miss His presence, power, and plan to bring good out of every situation.

What is it going to take for you to start calling on God instead of a friend or Fritos?

2. Release your pain, problem, mental processes, or predicament to God.

To understand the level of trust God requires here, think about the last time you sold a car or maybe even a house. After the final transaction, where you handed over the keys to the new owner with no strings attached, what was your level of emotional, physical, or financial involvement with it? If you actually released it completely, did you still check on the level of care, the loan balance, or interior cleanliness? Of course not! You didn't own it anymore. This is the level of trust God is seeking from you as you *release* your cares to Him.

We will talk more about this later, in the section about breaking through blockages, but sometimes the reason something is especially hard to release is because it is what I call a "layered issue." Like peeling an onion, you've got to work past the outside levels of self-protection to get at the real source of tears.

I was recently faced with a major challenge that I quickly released to God, but I couldn't get freedom to progress, because the next thought was another problem. I actually grabbed a worksheet (see Appendix II, "The 4R Worksheet," for blanks) and filled out 23 line items I needed to individually release to God before I came to peace about the original problem. Like a big ball of twine in my mind, every released challenge exposed the next unsolved problem in relationship to the overall issue.

It took less than 15 minutes for this major healing to occur, and I was able to release it all. In exchange, I received faith and joy coupled with surprised delight: I didn't even know all that junk was inside me, and now it was all gone, thanks to this latest exercise in release.

In the end, I think we will come to thank God for every challenge because each exposes an opportunity for spiritual healing. Envision yourself at spiritual boot camp, willing to exercise the new skill of releasing your problems to God as each comes up.

3. Receive His choice of exchange gifts for you (often peace, hope, faith, or comfort).

The only way to fully receive, appreciate, and enjoy God's help through the crisis, is by pausing after release long enough to receive the exchange gift God wants to apply to your life in that moment.

Practically everyone misses this step, yet it is the critical step for experiential joy. In fact, if you know a God-lover who struggles with sadness, it might be because she has never understood how to pause before action to receive God's exchange gift.

> God wants our problems and is able to solve them without our help.

We are all in the habit of solving our own problems. Like two-year-old tyrants, we want to do it ourselves, our way. In addition, after releasing our problem to God, our most typical habitual response is to take it right back. We can barely fathom the fact that God wants our problems and is able to solve them without our help.

Remember to be still, to pause long enough after release to understand and receive your exchange gift from God.

Marnie Swedberg

True Release Requires Faith

Trusting God can feel, well, downright irresponsible. This is one of the biggest reasons I still frequently fail to trust God—I hate this feeling, the sense that I'm being lazy or irresponsible! So, I take action myself. Even though I've seen God provide for me, time and time again for decades, I try to solve my own problems.

Letting God carry me is much better! Let me share two examples:

- When our daughter traveled alone from our home to British Columbia, Canada, by train, bus, and ferry, we lost touch with her for over 32 hours. This was before cell phones, so her only opportunities to call were at transfer locations.

    There was an especially tricky connection which, if missed, would have left her alone in the Seattle bus depot overnight. This concerned me because she was a beautiful, sheltered, 17-year-old girl, from a small town in northern Minnesota.

    As you can imagine, every hour past the Seattle transition point was torture for me! I paced, I prayed, I cried out to God, but not understanding the third R, I did not know how to truly release my concern.

    At some point close to 30 hours, I was nearly frantic, knowing every passing hour a person is missing reduces the chances of them being found alive. I was pacing and praying when I saw a picture in my mind of Keren calling me from a phone booth in Seattle to tell me she was fine.

    That comforting picture then changed, shocking me as I saw in the vision a man behind her with a knife. I understood that, as soon as she hung up the phone, he was ready to stab or steal her.

In my heart I heard this message, "Marnie, even if Keren calls you, it will only mean she is safe for that moment. Neither her call to you, nor your worry, are helpful. Trust Me!"

At peace, I waited. Keren eventually called. She was fine. The transfers had been too tight for her to both catch her next ride and call; she'd opted for the safety of the rides, and she was calling now, as soon as possible, OK.

- Being small business owners in the restaurant and retail industries has been a precarious way to live since the recession of 2008. My husband, Dave, and I choose to live by faith, trusting God both for our needs and for what we do next. Still, we often find ourselves in desperate straights similar to those we faced a few weeks ago.

  As we sat down to pray, we clicked off seven things we desperately needed ASAP. The list went on, but the top four were:
  - $7,000 the next day for a payment. Money we didn't have.
  - Working vehicles because neither of ours were functional and we had no hope they could be anytime soon. It was the dead of winter, all local mechanics were overwhelmed with work, and our cars' problems required hours of research and labor. It wasn't looking hopeful, but we needed wheels.
  - Time to be two places at once the following day.
  - Dave's knee was giving out and he needed to be able to walk for work.

  The list was as ridiculous as it was impossible. No one could have guessed we were facing these challenges, except God.

  After praying, we went on our way and let God own the problems. Incredibly, looking back now, I see six out of seven are taken care of and the answer to the seventh is yet to be seen.

Marnie Swedberg

Does it feel responsible to let God handle our problems? No! Is it the most responsible thing in the world to let Him take care of things for us? Yes!

> We think we can do it without God or, worse, that God can't do it without us.

Our conflict is that we think we can do it without God or, worse, that God can't do it without us.

The third R, receive, provides the opportunity and time to deepen our trust in Him. I believe every trial positions us for a spiritual quantum leap if we choose to rest instead of rush ahead.

If you are curious as to how to understand the exchange gift God is giving to you, just quiet yourself and listen. In your heart, you will hear a response that will comfort, shock, or even amuse you. One hint is that it's usually not what you would think in that circumstance if left to your own devices. God's ways are much higher than yours.

Don't overly fret about comprehending these communications right away. Again, in similar fashion to how a baby learns to understand language, it may take a little while for you to hear anything at all, and possibly longer for you to trust it is God speaking to your heart. Just start where you are today and proceed by faith.

4. <u>Respond</u> with a "Thank You" and a willingness to assist.
The fourth R is possible only if you've successfully completed the first three. It's a final exam and here is your easy-to-score, pass/fail test:

> Pass – You arrive at the fourth R at peace. You don't have a problem anymore because you've given it to God and you are free to say thank you to the One who freed you from it.

Fail - You arrive at the fourth R feeling anything but grateful. You are still in possession of a huge problem. You are not able to do this step because your brain is in fix-it mode instead of conduit mode. (I'll go into this more later, but here it's important to begin defining the word "failure" as "feedback." More about this in Chapter 9.)

If you need to, go back and repeat any missing "Rs" until you are virtually bursting with gratitude toward God. When you truly release it to God, and receive His replacement gift, you find yourself at peace and able to say a heart-felt, hands-off, "Thank You!"

Thanking God releases the power of heaven on your behalf. You don't have to thank Him for the problem, but He does ask you to thank Him as He carries you through it. What I've come to appreciate is that we'll end up thanking Him for everything—even the most painful challenges we have ever endured.

Remember my blind friend, Janet? She is a master flow through vessel and a glowing example of God's love to everyone she meets.

Janet went blind at age 31. Her husband, in his grief, fell for another woman. Janet found herself blind, rejected by her husband, and alone with their three small boys. In her darkness and despair, she met God. Jesus changed her life. She is a vibrant and beautiful, available flow through vessel for God.

God's love through her healed her broken heart, bound up her deep despair, and won back her husband. They've now been married for 39 years.

In addition to their previous challenges, Janet and her husband walked through every parent's worst nightmare: Their 19-year-old son was murdered, stabbed 23 times. Even worse, after the torture of a lengthy trial, the killer was found "not guilty" on all charges despite overwhelming evidence of his guilt.

Janet says, "We were devastated. We went home distraught. That night we had no idea what else to do, so we knelt together and prayed and forgave that man."

Janet, still blind, travels the world, alone with God, sharing a message of hope, love, and forgiveness with everyone she meets.

This is what it looks like to be a flow through vessel for God—living out the 4Rs in the face of every trauma and tragedy life throws at you. It's God's life flowing through yours, and it's amazing!

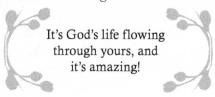

It's God's life flowing through yours, and it's amazing!

How to Move Toward Relationship Joy with God

God has a wonderful sense of humor, which is one of my favorite parts of our relationship. Upon hitting the fourth R, I am calm, delighted by that fact, and totally dependent on His intervention to bring even one encouraging thing out of whatever mess I am facing now.

After recognizing, releasing, and receiving His exchange gift, I get playful. Remember, I just gave Him the problem I would otherwise be ripped up about for hours, days, or longer. I usually say something like this:

- Thank You, God!
- [Winking], I see you now have a HUGE new problem on Your hands.
- [Teasingly], I wonder if You're up to it?
- [Honestly], Is there anything I can do for You just now?

Here, and only because I am clear of all the negative emotions surrounding the issue I just brought to Him, I become a flow through vessel and can actually sense, hear, or understand what to do. Sometimes I am to go on with my day as if nothing happened, while other times He prompts me to take some particular action toward the resolution of the original problem.

Most often, what He puts in my heart seems so silly and small in comparison to what I just off-loaded onto Him, it makes me laugh and I am happy to get right at it. Frequently, His request of me has nothing even remotely to do with the problem I gave Him, but rather has positioned me to be a grateful conduit for whatever He needs to do in, to, and through me next.

God Comes to Your Rescue:
Your Basic 911 Crisis Responses to Learn

> God's goal for you is total dependence on Him.

Remember how we said that calling on Jesus is the spiritual equivalent of dialing 911?

I recently experienced something so painful it took several minutes for me to stop saying, "Jesus, Jesus, Jesus..." I could not stop until God gave me a thought that allowed me to move into the second R, Release, and beyond.

Sometimes it is even harder than that. Have you ever heard of someone falling down the steps and lying there a long time because they couldn't reach a phone to call for help? When this happens to me spiritually, I can't even handle the two "911" syllables in the word Jesus. I just say, "God, God, God, God..." in rapid succession until I can transfer my mind to Jesus.

Don't worry! Life can be downright traumatizing, but with God helping you, it's going to be OK.

Marnie Swedberg

When God's Request Doesn't Make Sense

God's goal for you is total dependence on Him. Whenever anything except the blood of His love is flowing through your spiritual veins, you are not fully functioning. It's the dif-

God can use every problem for good.

ference between being a wig and healthy, thriving hair, or being a piece of lumber instead of being a living, growing tree. The sooner you quit trying to be a god and let God flow through you, the sooner you will experience true freedom and joy.

After completing the "Thank You" phase of the fourth R, your next step is to extend an offer to assist God as He deems best.

Now really, be honest: What could you possibly do for God that He couldn't do without you?

But God... I love that phrase! God has chosen to use you. In His plan, He's made it reasonable to partner with Him and actually please Him by allowing Him to flow His life through yours. Simply do whatever He asks of you, trusting Him for the directions, resources, and opportunities to complete it.

God can use every problem for good.

Problems are prime real estate for perfecting trust. Don't' slash the value of your challenges by selling out to the first solution you see. Instead, wait for God to flex His muscles for you. His goal is your dependence, not your productivity.

Section III

Reality Check

Chapter 6
Stop Being Abused By Life & Start Being Used by God

*Y*ou are serving as a flow through vessel for food, water, and oxygen, but also for ideas, thoughts, and emotions: Slogans shock you, friends fail you, and family members unwittingly file their day's trash in your mental portfolio. Every last piece of information flows to you, whether you're ready or not. It then flows through you, instantly or over time, as you emotionally process it all.

You are an emotional, relational, and spiritual flow through vessel created by God for good. If it's not His love flowing through your spiritual veins, then it's an inferior fuel source and it's polluting your life, causing avoidable stress.

> You are serving as a flow through vessel.

The two types of flow throughs are direct and metamorphic and the following self-test will help you identify what you currently do when flooded with emotions that must flow through somehow.

Self Test: Current Flow Through Status

Complete each statement below to reflect your typical response. If none of the options apply, write in your own. If you're not sure how to answer, imagine what your best friend would choose for you if she was taking this test on your behalf.

1. When someone says something hurtful to me:
   a. I verbally spit something similar back at them. (DFT)
   b. I breathe a prayer and respond to them with God's heart. (DFT)
   c. I submerge my reactive thoughts, feeding my dis-ease. (MFT)
   d. I breathe a prayer and mix together God's heart with my own emotions to deliver a less than lethal response. (MFT)
   e. I…

2. When I receive bad news:
   a. I release it, as is, into my database of historical bad news. (DFT)
   b. I release it to God, as is, for Him to care for on my behalf. (DFT)
   c. I add or multiply previous bad news of its same type to arrive at an even greater pain level than the current news merits. (MFT)

    d. I mix my owns fears and frustrations with my faith, providing at least some buffer for my brain. (MFT)

    e. I...

3. When I suffer pain:

    a. I identify the pain, address it with appropriate actions (possibly pain meds, a doctor visit, etc.), and move forward as best I can. (DFT)

    b. I give the pain to God, as it is, asking for His instructions. (DFT)

    c. I amplify the pain by focusing on it, complaining about it, sharing it with others, and/or feeling sorry for myself about it. (MFT)

    d. I combine my awareness of God's presence with my intense focus on the pain. It's not the same as giving the pain to God, but it does lessen its intensity. (MFT)

    e. I...

4. When I am unclear about what to do, or baffled by an outcome I didn't expect:

    a. I begin asking for advice in every way I know how. (DFT)

    b. I go directly to God for advice and counsel. (DFT)

    c. I translate my confusion into self-deprecation, fear, or even depression. (MFT)

    d. I go to God, but mostly can't hear Him due to my confusion. (MFT)

    e. I...

5. When I am reminded of past mistakes I've made:
   a. I punish myself again each time, as if I am reliving the mistake. (DFT)
   b. I remind God that He's forgiven me and I'm free from guilt and shame. (DFT)
   c. I compound my pain each time I remember a past failure, combining it with other previous failures, including their negative emotions. (MFT)
   d. I combine a weak sense of forgiveness with the strong sense of guilt. (MFT)
   e. I...

You can't avoid being a flow through vessel. It is a constant reality in your life. The only way to stop the flow is to die, which is why, unaware of other options, you can fall for temporary relief by giving in to a favorite habit or addiction.

The great news is that God has a radically better plan for us: He created us to be His flow through vessels and offers us a transcendent peace that makes truffles or tranquilizers seem ridiculously ineffective by comparison.

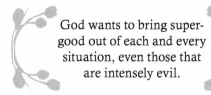

God wants to bring super-good out of each and every situation, even those that are intensely evil.

The beauty of being God's flow through vessel is that His love transforms every situation into something better than it could be without Him. Unmet expectations lead to a happy surprise or the loss of a loved one to a deeper dependence on God. You personally benefit from every experience with God, whether it's obvious or not. His presence also enables you to provide encouragement and help to the others involved.

I believe God wants to bring super-good out of each and every situation, even those that are intensely evil.

1. When someone says something hurtful to you, give it to God, receive His replacement gift in exchange, and find yourself sharing His love with your attacker.

2. When you receive bad news, quickly release the news, your emotional response, and its eventual outcomes to God, receiving peace for yourself and all involved.

3. When you suffer pain, go through it with Jesus. Not only will the Ultimate Pain Reliever address your discomfort, but you'll find yourself being used to encourage those around you, even in the midst of your personal trauma.

4. When you are unclear about what to do, or baffled by an outcome you didn't expect, go directly to God for advice and counsel. There is no need for confusion to trouble you, rather you can employ curiosity, being inquisitive instead of worried about how God will take care of you this time.

5. When you are reminded of past mistakes you've made, recall how God has completely forgiven you and how free you are from guilt and shame. Astoundingly, you will find yourself extending that same level of love and forgiveness toward those who are dragging you through the dirt at the moment.

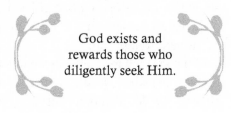

Your mission, should you choose to accept it, is to believe God exists and rewards those who diligently seek Him.

God exists and rewards those who diligently seek Him.

A new, amazing life is just around the corner for you when you do, because God already has the perfect plan and solution for every challenge you'll ever face.

God's Creative Stress Management Plan

I hosted a club in my home for 10 years for girls between 11 and 18 years old. We would meet one to three afternoons a week, from 3:00 to 5:30 PM, to make meals for families in precarious situations such as the loss of a loved one, medical trauma, moving, or bringing home a new baby.

As you can imagine, being alone in the kitchen with a dozen inexperienced cooks was quite a challenge. Ensuring the meals were edible was the ultimate trick.

There were times when I would reach the end of myself. Whether needing more patience, love, ideas, or you-name-it, I'd run out.

When we rely on our own strength, we do run out!

In those moments, I would turn my body away, sometimes opening the refrigerator or a cupboard, and pretend to search for something. Mentally looking up, I'd pray. I'd say something like, "God, I am out of _____ (whatever) for _____ (whomever)! *I need some of Yours right now.* Thank You."

As I'd turn back around, inevitably something shifted in the environment to help me receive God's provision. Sometimes the doorbell or phone rang. Other times someone made a joke or started to tell a story. Once a girl actually dropped a 9x13" pan of prepared dessert on the floor, upside down, right then, as I returned from prayer.

What amazed me, and still amazes me, is that God is willing to intervene when we ask. His response may be as simple as the ringing of a doorbell or as unsettling as a pan of perfectly good food now wasted on the floor. Whatever He chooses to use to answer our prayers, He does so because He cares.

I can't always say, "I would have done it that way," but I can always say, "God was here."

Every time God has used me as a flow through vessel, He has had His reasons. Quite frankly, much of the logic and necessity of doing

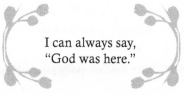

I can always say, "God was here."

things His way is above my pay grade, but that seems reasonable to me, since He is God and I'm not. So I trust Him with childlike faith to the best of my ability in each moment.

I'm excited to invite you to continue with me farther along on this amazing journey of becoming God's flow through vessel and living the life He created us to enjoy.

Created Intentionally

Do you believe in evolution? Both creation and evolution require an act of faith. I think it takes way more faith to believe in evolution than in a loving, Creator God because everything I see points to intelligent design, including cycles of birth, life, and death. The complexity of nature is mind-bending with nearly eight million species of animals and insects alone, plus predictable seasons, twenty-four-hour days, and the ability to time Olympic competitors down to the one-thousandth of a second.

In nature I see evidence of deterioration: cars rust, fabric fades, and living things die, while evolution requires continual improvement.

If evolution is true, and there is no God, then there is no one to whom we must give account for ourselves. This is an inviting concept for those who choose to live lives focused on self-gratification at the expense of others.

If, however, there is a God, then not only does He have a vested interest in your life, but He built you in a particular way and holds your unique instruction manual. He longs to be your Best Friend, your Benefactor, and your go-to Source for everything you ever need.

I invite you to consider the following questions.

The Uniqueness of You

1. Who strung together your three billion base pair of DNA in your particular way?
2. Who orchestrates the synergy enjoyed by your body's 50 trillion cells?
3. Who taught your eyes to blink 10 million times a year?
4. Who figured out how to move one red blood cell through all 60,000 miles of your arteries in less than 20 seconds?
5. Whose design causes your conscious mind to process up to 40 stimuli per second and your subconscious mind to process up to 20 million stimuli in that same second?
6. Who decided at what precise time you would enter the world?
7. Who decided if you would be an American, Egyptian, Italian, or Mongolian?
8. Who assigned you your parents?
9. Who decided who would be your siblings and which birth order you'd enjoy?
10. Who decided your height, bone structure, eye color, hair color, and skin tone?
11. Who gave you the mental capacity you enjoy today?

12. Who determined your natural learning style?
13. Who orchestrated the unique learning opportunities you've experienced?
14. Who blended your personality into the exact mix that makes you unique?
15. Who will decide at what moment and in what location you take your last breath?

These are a few examples of things proving you are an exclusive, one-of-a-kind design. You are not necessarily smarter, stronger, or better looking than your ancestors, but you are definitely more sophisticated than a cell phone or automobile. No one would say these could have evolved no matter how many million years we gave them.

Everything we enjoy has been designed by someone and has usage requirements. For example, a Corvette. If you run sludge through the engine, you have an expensive piece of junk. You may be able to collect money from a salvage shop for parts, but it would never be what it was created to be. It could never do what its designers planned it to do.

Same with you! Without the engine of God, without His love flowing through you, you are not experiencing the life God intended for you. Without God at the core of your being, you will always fall short of your potential.

> **Without God at the core of your being, you will always fall short of your potential.**

You are uniquely designed by God to need God—not only as an external source of help, like a Santa, banker, or personal assistant, but as your internal source, *your fuel*, with the energy of His life flowing through your spiritual veins.

It's Time to Trust God

God not only created you, but He created time. All of history is actually "His Story." He is personally outside of time and space. He existed before time, creating time for our benefit: Time to get to know Him, time to learn to love Him, and time to become a master flow through vessel for Him as He introduces Himself to every person on earth, some through you.

Time is an interesting thing. From this day forward, whenever you think of the date, remember that time was God's idea and revolves around Jesus Christ.

BC means "Before Christ" and refers to the years before Jesus Christ was born of the virgin Mary. AD, "Anno Domini" in medieval Latin, is translated as "In the year of our Lord," referring to the year of Jesus' birth.

The most important decision you'll ever make is to spend time with God. Talk to Him as you fall asleep at night and greet Him before you open your eyes in the morning. Learn to listen and value His input all day long. Trust Him completely and invite Him to flow through you. This is the prescription for the best life possible both here and for eternity.

If you feel sort of overwhelmed at the thought of being in constant contact with God throughout your busy days, or embarrassing ways, compare your spiritual relationship with God to a dolphin's physical dependence on air.

Breathing the Air of Prayer

Dolphins are water dwellers but air breathers. They were created to live under the water, but if they don't breathe air every few minutes, they die. They go up for air constantly, without ceasing, while living their lives underwater.

You and I are earth dwellers, but prayer breathers. We
thrive spiritually by going up
to God for air through prayer.
Without the air of prayer, we
die spiritually.

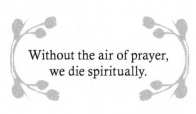

**Without the air of prayer,
we die spiritually.**

God is always with us, but when we fail to bring Him into our
conscious awareness through prayer, we gasp for air, grasping
for anything we feel may help, until we find ourselves addicted
to God-substitutes instead of being dependent on Him.

I can't pray all the time, not every minute, but I do pray constantly. I never quit praying: Life events coupled with my emotional responses serve as my reminders, like a dolphin's need for
air forces it to the surface.

Do I feel happy? I thank God! Sad? I ask for perspective.
Convicted? I ask for forgiveness. Hurt? I pray for healing.
Embarrassed? I laugh over it with God. Too busy? I seek direc-
tion. Exhausted? I pray for rest or added energy.

In your relationship with God, you are invited to receive help
from God at all times just like a dolphin can tap into oxygen
with one simple action. Here's how life can be for you:

- Go up for air constantly, pray without ceasing. Share your
  every high and low with the God who longs for this level of
  relational dependence. He is your spiritual air. You access His
  air through prayer.
- Whenever you feel happy, leap free of the waves of life and just
  play with God. No kidding! Tell Him a joke, sing a song, dance
  a jig, and enjoy your Creator! It takes just a few seconds with
  Jesus to put life's problems back into perspective.
- Swim in a pod. Hang out with other God-lovers and
  work together toward your God-given goals. This fearless

partnership with God and His kids is your most powerful defense against any evil threat. Watching you laugh in the face of fear, trust when the threats are in high gear, and choose faith when your hope should be gone, these acts of faith dishearten your spiritual enemies and send them to seek easier targets.

It is possible to do your life without the air of prayer, but it's impossible to do God's life without it. As you breathe the air of prayer, God flows His life and love through you, creating eternal value with every breath.

I believe that taking out the trash, as God's conduit, has an eternal reward, while feeding the poor without Him is only as helpful as it is in the moment. It is helpful in the moment, but it lacks the flow of God, therefore it lacks eternal value.

The Bible makes it clear that there is a fiery furnace set up to test all of our works. Our admittance into heaven is not based on works, but on our trust in Jesus' death on the cross to save us from hell. However, every last thing we've done in life will go through this fire:

- Anything accomplished independent of God will burn and be gone. The Bible calls these things wood, hay, and stubble. If you've ever wanted to start a great fire, these are the fodder you'd choose.
- The things done by God through us, as He flows through our lives, are called gold, silver and precious gems. These pass through the fire, perfected by it, directly into eternity with us.

Because I have come to appreciate the eternal value of my life and work here, I care very little about social validation, a big bank balance, or writing a best-selling book. In fact, my entire focus and motivation for living, my one reason for getting out of bed in the morning, is to love and yield myself to this great God, all day, every day, as I work and play.

My heart, my goal, my breath is to let God flow through me. Due to this powerful perspective, I stay alert for thoughts, situations, or temptations that threaten my spiritual air supply. At the earliest hint of trouble, like a tingly faucet, I recognize the need to go up for air through prayer.

Why wait until you are doubled over in pain, and under so much strain you can't think straight? Instead, learn to quickly and consciously run into the presence of God, through prayer. His power and perspective serve as a mental and emotional "reset" button allowing you to return to your present situation, ready to do life God's way.

An arrow prayer is fine, but whenever you can, quickly pray through the 4Rs:

> **Recognize** you're in trouble and God wants to help by flowing through you.
>
> **Release** any anxieties.
>
> **Receive** God's exchange gift, which is often simply the ability to breathe again—peace.
>
> **Respond.** Tell Him thanks for the stress-relief, thanks for the air, and thanks for Jesus who bothers to care. Offer your assistance to Him at His discretion.

The more often you feel the need for prayer, the better! The goal is to create a new habit of God-dependence, so the

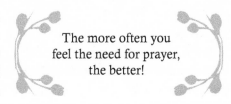

The more often you feel the need for prayer, the better!

more practice you get, the more quickly you develop into a master flow through vessel, the most enjoyable life possible.

Why Jesus?

Have you ever wondered why Christians are always talking about the need to come to God through Jesus? I mean, shouldn't it be true that anyone can come to God any which way they choose? Shouldn't a Buddhist be able to connect to God through Buddha? Shouldn't a nice person expect a warm welcome into God's kingdom even if she has never understood the need for Jesus as Connector?

This concept of "only one way to God" seems to trip up a lot of people. It feels somehow offensive that God requires something specific from us if He is truly loving.

But God knows we expect Him to be both nice and fair.

God is good, ultimate good, so He can't always be "nice." We know this instinctively because if one of our earthly judges lets a murderer go free, without penalty, we condemn that judge. It is justice or niceness, but not both.

> God is good, ultimate good, so He can't always be "nice."

We know that it is not fair for people to steal, cheat, lie, or kill and get away with it. We learned this from God. God both made the rules and created our need for them.

To develop the argument that God should be allowed to require "one and only one" connection method, simply observe how things work here on earth. Take this true or false test to identify if you've found this to be the case in your life.

Self Test: The "Appointment" Test

T   F   If I have a great idea that is 95% sure to result in world peace, I can call the White House and get an appointment with the President. He is happy to meet with me.

T   F   If I want to get an appointment to be interviewed by Oprah about my wonderful, tragic, or heart-warming life story, all I need to do is talk to any of her people, and they can get me in.

T   F   If I need a loan, I just walk into any bank and up to any loan officer and ask him for one. Every loan officer I ask will give me a loan, regardless of my financial qualifications.

T   F   If I need my car fixed, I swing by the repair shop, and they fit me right in. I'm their top priority, because I have a need for them, and that's their job. No charge!

T   F   Whenever I get pulled over for speeding, I simply explain my reason for going fast this time, and they let me off. They are completely understanding and gracious.

T   F   When I go to an amusement park or big concert, I explain that I don't think it's really fair for them to charge such high admission fees, and, being the loving, understanding people they are, they let me in for free.

T F If I want my haircut and walk in without an appointment, my beautician stops caring for the current client and gives me my due respect by cutting my hair perfectly, immediately, and free of charge, of course.

I mean, even if you were dying, you wouldn't lay at home in your bed expecting a doctor to magically show up, cure you, and charge you nothing. You'd at least call 911 or go to an emergency room. Once there, you'd agree to pay whatever it cost to get the cure.

Yet when God invites us into an instantly accessible, 100% free-to-us relationship with Him through Jesus, we balk because we think it sounds unfair or somehow unreasonable.

As a culture, I fear we've become so proud as to believe God should let us decide how we connect with Him. And when it comes to heaven, based on many funerals I've attended, it appears that dying is the only prerequisite we think is fair as an entry ticket into His personal home.

But what if God is God? What if His availability to us is dependent on something?

What if God is God?

We can't even take a geometry class without first taking algebra, and the God who created us is far more powerful than an educational adviser, hairdresser, or highway patrolman. In order to become who God created us to be, we have to come to Him on His terms, connecting with Him, through Jesus Christ.

God Sent Jesus for Us

God is perfect. Heaven is His home—it, too, is perfect. We are imperfect. On our own, we can't go: We'd ruin it!

Marnie Swedberg

It is because of His love that He made a way for us to come close to Him through Jesus Christ. It is so simple that many refuse to believe it as truth.

He asks us to believe He exists and loves to reward those who seek Him. He asks us to admit that we are imperfect and need His help.

Admitting imperfection should be easy for anyone! Who isn't flawed? Yet, incredibly, this is the point where many people walk away saying, "How could God ask me to admit my guilt? That's demeaning."

A human judge cannot let a criminal go without consequence, and God is the Ultimate Judge. He cannot ignore, overlook, or give us a "pass" for any of our failures, and we have thousands. He can and does, however, accept a suitable substitute. Jesus willingly served the sentence for us. He was the perfect God-man, and He came to die in our place.

Have you watched *The Passion of the Christ* yet? That movie is a pretty realistic rendition of the physical torment of Jesus' last hours, persecution, and crucifixion. What the movie couldn't portray was the broken-hearted Father, who watched in agony and commitment as His Son intentionally died for the sins of the world. Nor could it possibly communicate the cost to Jesus of leaving heaven for 33 years.

If Jesus didn't need to die, why did He? If God didn't need Jesus to go through all that suffering, why would He allow it? Either there is a compelling reason, or they are stark raving mad. No parent would stand by silently and let evil men kill their child unless there was no other option.

God loves you. That's the only reason Jesus came to earth, lived a perfect life, and allowed Himself to die in your place. It was an intentional choice and the motivation was His love for you.

Truth

God loves everybody! He loves you, the murderer, the child molester, and even the God-hater. It is not a matter of whether or not God is love, it is a matter of equity. Whoever comes to God by faith in Jesus Christ receives forgiveness and pardon, period. It has nothing to do with performance, and everything to do with love.

God loves you.

God's love and Jesus' blood covers all your sin, enabling you to relate to God in a personal way. He invites you into His family: Father, Son, Holy Spirit, and you. They've chosen to have a relationship with you. They can hardly wait to flow pure goodness and grace through your spiritual veins every day of your life if you will humble yourself and admit your need.

If you've never truly understood or accepted this before, receive it now:

1. Come to God with nothing but faith.
2. Ask Him to forgive you, for Jesus' sake.
3. Receive His gift of the Holy Spirit to live inside you.
4. Let the rest of your life be a "Thank You" for this gift.

In the following pages you'll discover how to remain an open-hearted vessel for all God desires to flow to and through you. You'll learn how to quickly identify and remove any blockages that threaten His flow, and you'll come to enjoy the results of God's life in and through you both now and for eternity.

Section IV

Habit Mastery

Chapter 7
Move Forward
One Step at a Time

When it comes to habit formation or cessation, it is critical for you to understand how marvelously God has created your brain. Your conscious mind is processing about 40 stimuli per second and your subconscious mind over 20 million in the same second.

The engine of your subconscious is processing data 24/7, 365 days per year at the staggering rate of a billion stimuli per week. It maintains records of everything you see, feel, touch, or hear; every action, decision, and failure; and every thought, hope, and dream. These sensations are documented, and when a thought or action is regularly repeated in response to a certain trigger, it becomes a habit or addiction, creating deep ruts in the roads of your subconscious. It becomes your natural response.

Balance

One of the key roles of the subconscious mind is to retain balance in the body. When you get hot, it kicks on the sweat glands to cool you

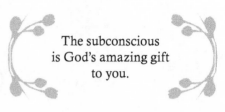

The subconscious is God's amazing gift to you.

down. When cold, it sends blood to the skin's surface, causing goose bumps to raise your body temperature. When you slip while walking, it sends your arms outward to balance you.

The subconscious is God's amazing gift to you, managing those 50 million cells, 60,000 miles of arteries, and 10,000 blinks per year with rarely a need to bother your conscious mind at all.

But when you propose a habit change, you threaten system balance, and the subconscious cannot allow it. Life coaches call this phenomena "self-sabotage" because it appears you are fighting against your own best interests. In fact, the subconscious is doing exactly what God created it to do: forcing you to slow down and drive toward your goal at a safe and sane speed.

Think of your subconscious like a train with 100 cars speeding down a track:

- You are the one who instructed your brain-train to go in the direction it's been going.
- You convinced it this was a great direction with lots of benefits.
- You repeatedly reinforced this response, often with intense emotion attached.
- You are the only one who can request it to change directions.
- You need to give it reasons, and you need to give it time to slow down for the turn.

Ordering your massive brain-train to make a U-turn while going fast is going to fail. It knows it will derail.

The subconscious has a job: to retain life balance. It also has a plan. It knows that it is only a matter of time before some distraction will take your mind off the new idea, habit, or addiction-breaking goal, at which point it will quickly revert all systems back to status quo.

It's the old saying, "Don't rock the boat." Why? Because the entire boat may tip over. This is the position of your subconscious mind: Allow no change to deeply rooted routines.

You, for all your commitment to change, will eventually give in to your typical responses, because you have a limited number of stimuli per second to apply to so many conscious functions. Your habits rely on deeply ingrained, subconscious responses. It's like putting a 40 pound weakling into a boxing ring with a 20 million-pound sumo wrestler. The little guy's got no chance.

When distracted, you cannot help but fail to maintain your new standard, at least for a while, and when you realize your failure, you'll feel shocked and disappointed. You may respond by beating yourself up, making excuses, or quitting outright, but all three are overreactions to a predictable, God-implanted cycle.

Numerous research findings confirm what the Bible teaches: that the most effective method for habit formation or cessation is to select a ridiculously small, innocent-looking version of your full-blown goal and to master it before making any additional changes.

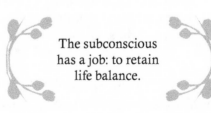

The subconscious has a job: to retain life balance.

An example from my own life was my desire to spend more time with God despite my busy schedule. I had failed multiple times trying to schedule rendezvous with God, each letdown followed by guilt and shame. (After all, it was God I was trying to fit into my schedule.) One would think He would take precedence over everything else, but it wasn't that easy.

Finally, I decided to adopt the habit of praying the Lord's Prayer before I opened my eyes in the morning. I would sometimes have to restart several times, due to falling back to sleep (again, how embarrassing), but the habit was simple and enjoyable enough that I found myself able to do it every single morning without fail. It was the perfect place to start— a micro habit.

Over time, I would keep talking to Him for longer and longer in the morning, discussing ideas, concerns, and thoughts as they toppled through my mind. As the joy of relationship grew, I found myself chatting with Him throughout the afternoon, too, until this little 30-second habit mushroomed into a life of prayer that continues to grow stronger even after 20 years.

The beauty of inviting God to change us is that we grow closer to Him along the way. He loves it when we trade out any part of a bad habit for Him. Just as flowers grow better in soil fertilized with manure, and rainbows show up only after thunderstorms, so God loves to use our bad habits to bring about His good.

God loves to use our bad habits to bring about His good.

Applying the 4R Response to our habits and addictions is more fun, less stressful, and includes less guilt and shame than any other approach. It's also extremely effective at enabling us to remain available as God's flow through vessels while in a far-from-perfect state.

As we invite God to gift us with love each time we face an emotional bump, He moves us gently from where we are to where we need to be. Some steps are barely perceptible, while others are quantum leaps.

Just start. By faith, step out and claim the name of Jesus or that first R of recognition as often as you can. Anytime you are able, add the second R of release, then receive His exchange gift and respond. Practice until these responses become your natural breath and God becomes your go-to in every situation.

Trusting God vs. Trying Harder

Years ago, a friend's daughter had a heart and lung transplant. Part of the recovery process was to take her off the ventilator for short stints, during which she had to relearn how to breathe, one breath at a time. Since we breathe in and out 20 to 40 times per minute, imagine how hard that was. Just try it for two minutes. It's nearly impossible to be consistent and be consciously aware of every single breath.

Before we can master the habit of breathing Jesus as our subconsciously driven response, we have to break the old habit of depending on ourselves and our personally preferred substitutes for God. This requires hard work.

So what differentiates trusting God from trying harder?

> **Trusting God is choosing to act in utter dependence on Him, while trying harder is opting to retain control.**

We retain control when we tell God how we are going to fix our problems. We trust Him when we relinquish ourselves into His choice of responses, expecting Him to flow through us.

Well-intentioned people become disillusioned, judgmental, or religious in nature when they treat God like a to-do list or a project to complete. Walking with God is a relationship, not a religion. Brush your teeth religiously, but love God relationally. Don't "do devotions" and then ignore God the rest of the day! God loves it when we come to Him humbly, honestly, and often.

Don't be proud. Instead, delight in the fact that you can't fail Him. Like a four-year-old bringing his mom "flowers," God values your dandelion-love while rejecting your prideful attempts to impress Him.

Trust & Relationship

In a healthy, loving relationship, there is no need to "try harder" to earn the other person's love: They simply love you because they choose to love you. In response, you love them, too. This defines a healthy relationship.

God is love. His love is never dependent on what we do. Instead, He extends His love at all times, to all people, waiting only for us to respond to Him.

In our pride, we sometimes believe we can earn God's love. Not so! The only reason we love Him is because He first loved us. Our love is always reciprocal, while His is always initiating. His love cannot run out, while ours always does.

There is never any reason to "try harder" with God, only countless reasons to trust Him more.

> God values your dandelion-love.

Working Hard vs. Trying Harder

Although I never encourage "trying harder," I do champion the idea of working hard. I believe God created me to be a hard worker. In fact, I say He created me to be like a jet plane, flying fast and far or flat out on the tarmac, getting prepped for my next flight. Any pilot will tell you, planes don't idle well. Planes are built to fly; that's me!

Having said that, one of the most powerful habits I have mastered is to take one day a week off from work in order to rest. I include this example here because the Bible itself combines work and rest in ways that can be confusing.

It takes a ton of work for me to enjoy that day of rest. I sometimes arrive at a rest day exhausted from my effort to clear it. However, there are compelling reasons why I adopted this habit:

1. One of the 10 commandments requires us to take a "Sabbath" break every single week. God must have reasons. All His commandments are for our benefit.
2. God spent six days creating the world and then rested on the seventh. God models best practices: He took a rest after six days of work, and so should I.
3. In Hebrews the author actually says to "strive to rest."

So we see that striving to rest and trusting more are not quantitative. Both are about pressing further into who God is and the gifts He has already assigned to us, instead of trying harder to earn it or convince Him of our worthiness to receive it.

Pressing Into Freedom

The way God frees us is also not quantitative; it's progressive.

I best understood this when our family visited an amethyst mine in Thunder Bay, Canada. The beautiful purple strands of gemstone were barely

> Overcoming habits and addictions can take patient dependence on God and a willingness to be freed.

visible, woven through the giant wall of granite. Trapped between multi-ton layers of the lesser-quality stone, the gem was beautiful, but buried. It was fully amethyst despite being barely visible.

You are fully you despite any sin issues, bad habits, or harmful addictions hiding your true beauty. In the same way that mining amethyst takes time and patient effort, so overcoming habits and addictions can take patient dependence on God and a willingness to be freed.

The amethyst miner is a picture of God to me, because when I looked at that 70 foot long wall of granite, I couldn't see the amethyst, but he could. He said, "This wall will take about 70 years to mine." He said it with a smile and sense of determination. As he stood looking lovingly at the wall of granite, he felt no frustration with the amethyst for being stuck. I, however, was thinking, "Seventy years?! That's a lifetime!"

The miner was committed to doing things the right way as he freed the amethyst from the granite in which it was trapped. He said, "We can't use regular drills or jack hammers because they would damage the gem. We mine the amethyst using high pressure water guns."

God calls His Word the "water" of the Word. He says it is powerful to divide and separate. Do you see the analogy?

We are the amethyst, surrounded by stuff that needs to go away. God is like the amethyst miner, using the water of His Word to disentangle us from our junk. As weights, bondages, and addictions fall away, we are freed to be more fully ourselves in His presence and for His purposes.

It's not quantity; it's progress.

You cannot be any "more you" than you are at this moment. Yet as God frees you of your multi-layered sin issues, the eternal, redeemed part of you is exposed and able to enjoy and serve Him more fully. "More of you" for God, yourself, and others. More visible, available, and eternally useful, freer from the things that have made you feel trapped, ugly, or useless.

God Is a God of Process and Progression

Most counselors agree that there are normal progressions toward habit formation and cessation. When we walk with God by faith, He sometimes leads us through all the steps progressively, like an amethyst miner, and at other times He miraculously skips over some or all of the steps. The latter happened for me after my father's sudden death.

I learned of my dad's death in a difficult fashion. My husband, Dave, and I were at a buyer's show, twenty minutes from his home, when I noticed I had missed a call. I dialed my voicemail and heard this five-word message: "Marnie, your dad is dead."

As the shock waves of confusion and grief pummeled my mind, I habitually began grasping for God, repeating in my head, "Jesus, Jesus, Jesus!"

Over and over and over, almost without conscious awareness, I repeated the most powerful Name in the universe, as my mind short-circuited. We had just spent a week with my dad; he was fine! We were going to have dinner with him that night. He was at home. Did he have a heart attack? Maybe he went for a bike ride and got hit? How could he be dead?!

Yet just three or four minutes later, even before we got to our vehicle to drive to my parents' home, God planted an amazing, interruptive thought into my consciousness.

Out loud, I said, "Dave! If this is true, and my father is really dead, then he got his answer to prayer in spades!"

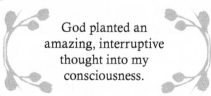

God planted an amazing, interruptive thought into my consciousness.

I cry again as I type this, because the moment was so incredibly comforting. Silently, I contemplated the words I had heard my father say so often—sentiments of not wanting to grow old to be a burden to others.

This sudden death was HIS answer to prayer, at our expense, but Dad's answer to prayer.

Did I grieve? Oh, yes. I was always "Daddy's Little Girl," and he was an amazing dad. I carried a physical pain in my chest for nearly six months. I also shed many tears of both joy and sorrow, and I still miss him.

I did grieve, but not the normal grief. God filled me with peace and hope. Every time grief came calling, I would render my emotions upwards in exchange for hope: hope for my dad because I knew he was exceedingly happy in heaven; and hope for me, as God walked me through every emotion of loss, gently and quickly.

I had learned the habit of calling on Jesus in times of pain, and just as God walked me through the grieving process with more peace than I could imagine possible, He longs to walk you through every habit change, sorrow, or joy from this day forward.

Dedicated Flow Through Vessels

When we choose to come to God, by faith in Jesus, He personally hooks us up to the continual flow of His life and love through His Spirit. He lives through us, pouring infinite ingenuity, skill, and resourcefulness from Him to us and through us to others.

Habits, however, can feel like discouraging God-stoppers. I call them chains of our own choosing, and they clobber us in two ways:

1. When we are falling into an addiction or habit pattern, we are lulled into complacency until we are stuck.

2. Once stuck, we are convinced that we should be able
    to get free anytime. We experience internal or external
    criticism for not being able to get unstuck.

But, it's not that easy.

Imagine a chain lying on the ground. When you engage in
your new behavior, it's like picking up the chain and wrapping
it around your ankles. No big deal! You can step out anytime.

As you repeat your behavior, it's as if the chain is winding
itself up your body, surrounding first your calves, then knees,
and so on. Still, no problem. Anytime you want to get free, you
unwind the chain. It's simple.

The problem comes when the chain entraps your hands and
arms. At this point, you are no longer able to unwind it yourself.
You are stuck. If you don't take action then, the chain continues
to wrap itself around you until it is up to your neck, then mouth,
nose, and eyes.

The fact that you chose the chain in the first place does not
guarantee you can reverse the choice anytime you wish and be
free. More often, God must personally unwrap you, one prayer
at a time.

Like a baby, you must learn to trust God as your loving parent, who desires to meet your needs with love and affection. The
gradual freeing from these chains of your own choosing is ideal
for this process.

Sure, we all know people who have been miraculously freed
instantly from a strong addiction, but God usually prefers to
transform us, little by little, one prayer at a time. He longs for
even our worst sins to become His opportunity to show us His
love. This is so different from expecting us to break a habit the
first moment He brings it to our attention; although, as mentioned, that is a possibility.

One night, after an intense series of events, I fell into bed exhausted and, in a not very nice voice, said to my Creator, "God! It's all out of control! EVERYTHING is out of control!"

His response was lightning fast and very funny. In my spirit, I heard His loving voice quietly say to me, "Marnie, out of *whose* control?"

We are all hopelessly addicted to the delusion that we are in control of anything.

Right! We are all hopelessly addicted to the delusion that we are in control of anything. The delusion is reinforced when we work independently to free ourselves from our habits and addictions, but our relationship with God is deepened every time we look to Him for help.

This section is about how to remove bondage-based habits and addictions so you can move forward toward the main goal of letting God flow through you all the time.

It always comes back to the same 4R Response.

Recognize something is threatening God's flow through you.
Release the emotion or problem to God.
Receive His exchange gift.
Respond with a "Thank You" and an offer to do whatever He asks next.

In my book, *Gasping for Grace: 31 Daily Devotionals for Discouraged Dieters*, I wrote:

I used to believe it was my job to abstain from sin.
I lived with that as my goal and obsession thus
was often overcome with grief and hopelessness.

Marnie Swedberg

Now I believe it is my job to focus on Jesus
and His ability to live through me.
When I sin, it is my job to believe for and receive
His forgiveness, just as I did the first time.

Perverted Faith

Everything in the world, from simple habit formation to rocket science--anything at all that eliminates God, is a perversion of His plan. God created us to be totally dependent on Him as He flows Himself, His love, and His goodness through our lives.

> God created us to be totally dependent on Him.

I remember well the first time God described me as a pervert. There was a moment when I actually felt convicted of being "perverted," and I can tell you, I was offended! I argued strongly that I was sure I was NOT a perverted person!

God corrected me. I was a pervert. I still am perverted whenever I change (change here means pervert) God's plans in order to satisfy some selfish desire.

I'm not alone in my perversion. At one point, during His life on earth, Jesus called His twelve apostles perverted. It was when someone complained to Him that the disciples had tried, but could not heal a little boy with seizures. Jesus demonstrated the frustration of God when He called them a perverse generation.

My question is this: How could He expect mere men to heal an epileptic child when, to this day, there is no cure for epilepsy? Yet when they failed, He called them perverted because Jesus, in dependence on God, had no trouble healing that boy. He had the power and connection, and was a pure flow through vessel.

The disciples tried really hard to heal that boy. God called that perversion because effort, when used as replacement for His power, is never the answer. Trusting more was what they needed to do, and that's what we need to do, too.

Again, I love how God uses superlatives. He talks about streets paved with gold, and here He attaches one of our most detestable words, "pervert," to a disciple's inability to heal an incurable disease due to lack of faith.

Wow! This still makes me shudder. It makes me more aware of how far I fall short of God's intended use of my life. I have a lot of growth potential; we all do. By nature, we'd typically translate even this small, corrective thought directly into guilt, shame, blame, or excuses. This, too, is a perversion God hates.

Instead, He invites us to yield up every thought, running through the 4Rs at every opportunity, as we continue to grow closer to the ownership of a faith capable of healing an epileptic. It's a slow process (no surprise there), but nothing is impossible with God, no matter how perverted or stuck we feel.

Chapter 8
The Amazing Process of Habit Formation

*M*ost habit creation and cessation attempts fail. They are driven by impatience, fueled by fear, and discontinued due to disappointment or despair.

Have you ever done this?

- Identify a bad habit.
- Decide to create a new habit.
- Fail within an hour, day, week, or month.
- Beat yourself up.
- Start again.
- Repeat, repeat, repeat.
- Give up and swear to never try again because it's too painful and doesn't work anyway.

Of course! Everyone has done this!

What's worse is that we translate the above scenario as failure, choosing to abuse ourselves and alienate our hearts from God instead of drawing closer to Him.

It's like we have a big report card in our heads: Successful attainment of a goal equals an "A+." Anything less ranges from a "B" to an "F," and we consider any temptation or actualization of the old habit to be an "F" for sure.

This is not God's way.

> **From God's perspective, your report card always reads "A+."**

First, from God's perspective, your report card always reads "A+" no matter what. No kidding! God sees you as complete and whole despite the fact that you are still trapped inside some bad habits. He sees you through the lens of Jesus—perfect.

Every failure—past, present, and future—falls under the umbrella of Christ's forgiveness and is a done deal. "A+" for you! So whenever you feel like a failure, it is not coming from God. God does convict of sin, but that is just the first of the 4Rs, your recognition of a problem. God has already forgiven the entire issue. He brings it to your attention only so you can receive His forgiveness and ask Him for your next step.

God does not expect you to master your habit the first time He brings it to your attention, or even the thousandth time for some habits. You might expect perfection, and others might pressure you toward it, but all that guilt, shame, and condemnation is not coming from God!

Imagine a kindergarten teacher, giving his class just one lesson on the ABCs and expecting perfection. Never! He'd give time, lessons, practice, and encouragement as each student mastered their ABCs in their own time and way.

God is your gentle, loving, habit-change teacher. The entire process was His idea, and He values every habit-related thought as an opportunity for you to grow closer to and more dependent on Him. Connecting with God as you practice your 4R responses *before* you hit the next trial, temptation, or tactical test is the key to faster freedom from them.

The more you practice in advance, the faster you'll soar to new skill levels.

Envision two buckets on the beach. The bucket on the left is full of sand representing your old, self-reliant, godless habit. The bucket on the right is nearly empty, representing the times you've chosen to fully depend on God and let Him flow through you.

There are two ways to move sand from the left to the right bucket:

1.   Make a God-honoring choice when faced with any temptation to ignore Him.
2.   Practice making those choices with God in your imagination before they arise.

Entrenched habits are hard to break because they are like deeply rutted roads in your subconscious. Neuroscientists estimate 95-99% of our 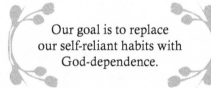 **Our goal is to replace our self-reliant habits with God-dependence.** everyday activities occur at the subconscious level. Fortunately the mind can adopt new habits fast when given ample opportunity to run the new route repeatedly, with energized emotion and hope.

Our goal is to replace our self-reliant habits with God-dependence. As we do, God Himself becomes our first go-to response in any situation. Just now, we grab a soda when we fill our gas tank, wipe out the sink after brushing our teeth, or retaliate with harsh words when offended. These responses are all based on habits.

Coming soon to your life are the new habits of grabbing for God when you feel threatened, wiping away other people's tears with His love instead of joining them in the pit of despair, and responding with grace instead of grumbling when offended.

If you have tried to break a bad habit to no avail, it can seem impossible because of how you've been going about it. Most people try to break bad habits with energy and emotion, using a direct frontal attack powered by motivation and will.

I believe the key is to stop trying harder and start trusting God more. This slow and steady approach, involving frequent use of the 4R Response, creates lasting change with a lot of pleasure and the least possible pain.

The 4 Reasons Habit Change Attempts Fail

Gravity is undeniable. We'd never just jump off a cliff without being sure there was deep water below or wings attached to our back.

In the same way, God has established many other rules, patterns, and processes that we need to embrace if we hope to succeed in life. Regardless of the habit you are trying to replace, and unless God chooses to miraculously heal you, there are four processes that can slow or stop your progress:

1. Tackling the habit before you are ready.
2. Tackling the habit head-on.
3. Tackling too much of the habit at once.
4. Upping the ante too soon.

1. If you tackle the habit before you are ready, you will fail, or at least, flip flop between success and failure indefinitely. Readiness is a requirement.

When a habit is too harmful for you to wait for readiness, it's best to enter a monitored program or detoxification center to break the addiction. These serve as external watch-dogs, isolating you from temptation for a set period of time, hoping you'll become ready to sustain change independently before you leave.

For all other habits, start and progress as soon as you can, employing trust in God for more readiness as time goes by. Go through the 4Rs every time you are tempted, have given in, or begin to think of engaging in the habit. Sometimes the best you'll be able to do is to ask God to help you "want to want to" develop a healthier habit. Do what you can, trusting Him fully.

2. Tackling your habit head-on is as pointless as rowing a canoe up the rapids. Unless it's a small habit, it is virtually impossible to sustain any progress for long, even if you feel really ready to do so. It's exhausting.

A primary role of the subconscious mind God gave you is to retain balance. When you change a habit, you jeopardize system balance; you threaten to capsize your canoe. You have grown accustomed to using your bad habit as a crutch, plus you had compelling reasons to adopt that habit in the first place, even if they were bad reasons. Now you need it. Like tree roots deep in the soil, which exist to help the tree weather wild winds that would otherwise topple it over, your habits are serving to help you maintain balance.

When you try to tackle your old habit head-on, your subconscious mind with its 20 million stimuli per second trumps your new goal at a ratio of 500,000:1.

Remember, your subconscious is like a train with 100 cars speeding down a track. Ordering it to make a U-turn while going fast is going to fail: It knows it will derail. The only way is to ask politely for a gentle, gradual turn. This loving, tender, patient approach succeeds every time.

3. Tackling too much of the habit at once is the most common death trap for habit change. While not requiring a full U-Turn, most of us are about as patient as a two-year-old, especially with habits we feel are dangerous or embarrassing. The brain, how-

ever, sees no difference. A habit is a habit. It's the default response to a set of circumstances, and the mind wants nothing to do with change. The brain will kick-back if you push too hard.

A habit is
a habit.

There are miracles, and there's also one predictable exception to this rule: trauma. If you happen to live through a massive heart attack, for example, your brain will readily allow you to change lifestyle habits fast. It instantly understands the impending threat of staying on the current track and is willing to let you threaten a derailment in favor of changing bad habits at record speeds.

Fortunately for us, God created a beautiful system for gently overcoming habits without the need for near-death experiences. The key is to agree to small, gradual changes, powered by our faith in God.

4. Upping the ante too soon is the final common mistake, and it is the number one reason you will get off track after

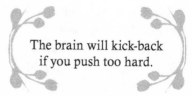

The brain will kick-back
if you push too hard.

making good progress. It's like speeding up your car while taking a sharp turn on glare ice: you'll spin out of control.

This trap is as easy to fall into as it is hard to avoid. After making progress, it can feel irresponsible to be content with small gains. You want to overcome this habit, and early success breeds a sense of power. You feel practically obligated to push harder, and why not? You are doing so well!

The problem is that the conscious mind is still not in control of anything.

Consider trying to break a big fist-full of spaghetti noodles. If you've got too many in your hand, it will be impossible; but when you reduce the size of the cluster, it's no longer even a challenge.

Habit strands are the same way. If you've been ignoring God since birth and are now 30 years old, you've got 30 years

> Our motto must be,
> "Non-resistant
> persistence."

x 365 days per year x maybe 100 or more ignores per day. That equals over 1 million ignore strands. Mama Mia! That's a lotsa spaghetti noodles to break!

Even after breaking dozens or hundreds of habit strands, you still have thousands remaining. All those raw noodles are rigid with sharp edges, keeping you trapped in your old habitual responses. The only thing you are going to be allowed to do is to break a few habit strands at a time.

As you envision a million godless habit strands that have created prison bars all around you, from the ground up higher than your arms can reach, remember that the habit becomes powerless one choice at a time. It's only power over you is due to the partnerships you have allowed. Again, "Chains of your own choosing."

Our motto must be, "Non-resistant persistence."

Think of the water in a babbling brook flowing its way down a mountainside. It comes to rocks, branches, and other obstacles along its way. It does not scream, yell, or demand that the obstacles move. It simply finds a way over, under, or around each.

Invite God to use the powerful water of His Word to gain the freedom He has already won for you.

You are actually already free! It's just a matter of coming into ownership of that freedom. Like a prisoner of war, after victory has been won, you might still be stuck behind bars in the prison camp where you've been living, but not for long. The planes are coming to take you home.

As you wait, break one or twenty habit strands at a time, keeping the faith and living as if your experiential freedom is due any day. Do not panic or sit idly and wait while you could be making progress. Do not lose hope!

Simply stay calm, stick with God, employ the 4R plan, and patiently move from trapped to free ASAP.

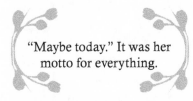

"Maybe today." It was her motto for everything.

As my nana always said, "Maybe today." It was her motto for everything: Maybe today God would answer that special prayer. Maybe today the anticipated check would come in the mail. Maybe today Jesus would return and take her home to heaven.

Practice, practice, and practice.

Practicing a new behavior in real-time is great, but practicing in advance is the most powerful tool in your spiritual tool belt. Life with God and habit formation is a process in which we and God both have roles to play.

I have this exercise I love to teach that helps internalize this reality. Would you do it with me right now?

Put your thumb and forefinger as close together as they can get. Really work at it until they are almost touching, but not quite. That's about the size of your part.

Now, stretch your arms out to both sides and extend your fingers out as far as you can. That is the size of God's part.

If our subconscious-to-conscious ratio is 500,000:1, I'm thinking our God-to-self ratio is probably even greater. God is exponentially superior to anything we think or know. He is a loving Father who gives us work to do, but it's all about relationship, not productivity. We get this so confused.

Not Always Fun or Fast, But Always Effective

I spent quite a bit of time as a youth with my left arm out of commission due to a growth plate break at age 11. Because I knew I had a problem, I went to a doctor. He said it would take surgery and physical therapy to fix my arm.

Because of my own and my parents' faith in the doctor and my willingness to follow his orders, 40 years later, I still have a functional left arm.

Was it easy? No! Was it fun? No! Did it hurt? Yes! Was it worth it? Yes!

Did I have a role in my cure? Yes! Did I cure myself? No!

> God is the great Physician and loving Father.

God is the great Physician and loving Father whose encouragement along the way can be misunderstood by His children: As He uses us to get His work done, we can come to feel very important indeed as pride wriggles its way into our hearts, when the only reason we experienced success was due to God.

In my book, *Feeling Loved: Connecting with God in the Minutes You Have*, I share the following analogy:

> This reminds me of preschooler, Johnny, whose father gets up early on a Saturday morning and says, "Want to help me build a shed today?"
>
> Little Johnny pulls on his overalls, straps on his toy tool belt, and heads to the back yard where he begins to "help" his dad. Pretending to saw, hammer, and drill all day, Johnny does more damage than good, asks a lot of questions, and slows his father down repeatedly.
>
> Yet, at the end of the day, Johnny's dad takes him by the hand and leads him back a pace or two to survey the finished shed. Side by side, with hands on hips, they sigh with satisfaction. Then Johnny's dad looks down and says, "Wow! You are such a big helper! Let's go get some ice cream!"

God carries us like this all the time. He lets us think we are really important and critical to the project, when in fact, the only thing He really wants is our love and companionship.

Chapter 9
Get Unstuck ASAP

We are designed to be God's flow through vessels to accomplish God-sized work in this world. In heaven, we will not have bad habits, addictions, or get stuck, but on earth we sometimes do.

If you have ever gotten your vehicle stuck in snow, mud, or sand, you're familiar with the strategy and effectiveness of rocking your car back and forth to gain enough traction to get free.

Every habit is either moving us toward or away from God. Yet like a broken elevator, a godless habit can lock us into place, stuck at one

> **Every habit is either moving us toward or away from God.**

level, with seemingly no ability to move up or down. The best way to get unstuck is to assign value to your habit: Every habit incidence, from pre-thought to temptation to action to confession, is an invitation for growth in your conscious awareness and dependence on God.

Did you catch that? Even the habits that are your worst nightmares have the potential to be your greatest growth boosters because every habit choice is an invitation for conscious awareness and dependence on God. In this one moment, do you want to move toward or away from God?

Godless habits stand like prison bars preventing you from intimacy with your Creator. Every time you feel stuck in a habit or addiction, whether thought or action, rock back and forth spiritually by calling on Jesus. After that, as soon as possible, kick into the 4Rs.

While I'd never encourage you to create new bad habits just so you can break them with God, it is a fact that your current addictions have the capacity to be your fastest path toward intimacy with Him. He is ready to prove Himself powerful to you in ways that will surprise and delight you.

A Little At a Time

Gaining freedom a little bit at a time is a biblical principle. When the Israelites were taking Canaan (called "freedom land"), they were to drive out the enemy a little at a time. God did not want them to take the whole land at once, because they wouldn't be able to maintain their progress.

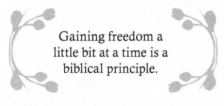

Gaining freedom a little bit at a time is a biblical principle.

To ensure you do not bite off more than you can chew, and to increase the likelihood you'll be able to maintain all the ground you gain, God will most likely heal you of your bad habits and addictions one little piece at a time, assigning you specific tasks along the way.

Marnie Swedberg

Our problem is that we are in such a big hurry! If we can't break the whole habit immediately, we give up in despair. Worse, we beat ourselves up for not being perfect. And then on top of that, we are faced with the consequences of the habit. It's a recipe for disaster, and we've made that recipe over and over. It's time to do this God's way!

How Habits Form

The seduction of a bad habit begins with one innocent-looking decision. It is super easy to break one spaghetti noodle, right? No big deal! It's when you've got too many that it becomes impossible to break all at once.

Habits are no different. In fact, until you can no longer easily break away, your habit is not viewed as a habit but as something you sometimes do. You don't know you are in trouble until you've lost the freedom to say "no."

For example, if you have been enjoying ice cream before bed since age four, and you're now 40, that is a habit nightmare of well over 10,000 individual habit strands. Gaining a

Fortunately, grace abounds!

21- or 60-day success streak is a good start, but it may surprise you how deeply rooted these long-held habits can be. In the end, each strand must be broken before you will no longer crave ice cream as your nighttime snack. Along the way, you may experience extended seasons of freedom (as you continue, with each evening of abstinence, to break more of the habit), but you may also fall back into it instantly when in a new surrounding, facing a certain feeling, or being with your family again.

Fortunately, grace abounds! You may experience freedom after consciously breaking only a few hundred or thousand strands of the 10,000 in existence. They do all have to go in order for you to experience real freedom, but the remaining several may fall away once their supporting strands have been removed.

Grace is interesting like that. Sometimes making a start at something is all that's required to gain the desired outcome. Grace protects in the opposite way, as well. Your body weight, for example, is established to protect you from unnecessary fluctuations. I don't know many people who monitor their intake down to the calorie, but eating just two extra TicTacâs per day should technically add 10 pounds to your weight every 10 years. The body is more forgiving than that!

When it comes to habit change, head the right direction and let the train turn in due time. Start with the small habit change of eating "less" ice cream each night—by a spoonful; or, if you usually eat a pint, consume only a cup and a half, thanking God as you put the rest back into the freezer for tomorrow night.

No matter what habit you are working on, you are actually replacing your bad habit with a better one—God dependence—and this plan works.

By the way, never, never, never try to break a bad habit without replacing it with a better one. In our ice cream example, don't just "skip" the bite(s); replace them with something. Ideally, replace them with something super healthy, like a mini-conversation with God, a bite of granola, or a swig of water with gratitude. Replace every habit with a better one! Include God in every choice.

Even just the act of being grateful is an excellent substitute: Express gratitude for the freedom to say "no, thank you" to that extra bite of ice cream before bed, knowing that soon you'll be free to take it or leave it all, free of any bondage to it.

Once you decide on a new, baby-step replacement habit, the fastest way to make progress is to practice your new habit before you get to the old-habit scenario. Like an Olympic gymnast reviewing her moves in her imagination before the big day, imagine yourself serving up the new, lesser amount of ice cream and engaging in its new, healthier replacement habit. Really pray, talk to God about it, and see it in your mind's eye.

Every time you envision yourself doing your new behavior in full color in your mind, you break a whole bunch of habit strands without even being tempted. When you add emotion to your mental images, such as gratitude toward God and delight at being able to accomplish this change, you break even more.

You will achieve freedom fastest when you do the majority of your habit-change work in the safety of your thoughts in the presence of God, without any visible temptation.

Regarding Miracle Cures

We all love miracle cures! Do you know that Americans spent nearly $61 billion last year on fad diets? What's really funny is that the miracle cure mentality is worldwide, but each culture has its own version of it.

When my husband, Dave, and son, Mark, traveled to the Philippines, they couldn't believe that people fell for the commercials selling instant growth. Filipinos don't want to lose weight, they want to gain height. The commercials there sell growth products, promising to add an inch to your legs if you buy their hocus-pocus cure.

We can't see the humor of our own folly until we see it in someone else. We are easy targets for offers including an instant fix to our pet peeve problem. This drive for quick fixes can lead to anger at God when He chooses to walk us through the healing process gradually instead of providing it instantly, because we know He could.

It's all in the perspective.

If you signed up with a sports trainer who gave you a set of daily drills and exercises to do, to develop your skills, you would readily submit yourself to his direction. God asks no less. His plan is to patiently break and remove habit strands, a few at a time, with Him, until you are free. As you walk through this process with God, your patience, faith, and love for Him grow while your godless habits shrink.

> God wants to use everything for your good.

Incredibly, God loves this plan! He created the mind to function in this way and is totally okay with us moving toward perfection one step at a time. Our steps may be giant-sized or barely perceptible, but either way, our freedom is won, one step at a time.

God wants to use everything for your good. Years ago I learned this phrase that helps me keep things in perspective:

Everything that comes into my life,
Satan wants to use to destroy me, but
Everything that comes into my life,
God wants to use for my good.

No matter what habit you are hating and no matter what you are doing, whether thinking of it, tackling it, giving into it, or you already gave in, apply the 4Rs as often and quickly as possible.

1. **Recognize** your habit. Recognition at any point breaks at least one habit strand.
   a. If you don't catch yourself until you're engaging in your bad habit, it's still better to recognize it then than never.
   b. The earlier you recognize what's going on and take action, the more strands you break. When you recognize and stop before you start, you break significantly more.

   c. Remember that realizing you are struggling is only the first part of the first R. The second component is to realize you cannot do this alone and God wants to help you.

   d. Pre-temptation practicing breaks the most strands possible—a big fistful. Practice your new habit in your mind with God as often as possible.

2. Release everything that has anything to do with your bad habit.

   a. When tempted, release your emotions and desires to God. Release your drive to engage in the bad habit and also your strong compulsion to overcome it by yourself without God. The Bible instructs us to avoid tempting situations and resist the devil, but does not teach us to resist temptation. In fact, it clearly states in James that you get a blessing when you endure trials and hardships, and it also says in Hebrews that God wants to comfort you through each temptation. Resisting is what Satan wants you to do. Trusting is God's plan for you, and it is the key to your habit cessation/creation success.

   b. Release to God your thoughts of shame, your self-abuse, or your excuses after any fall. Just come to God in your habit life the same way you came to Him at first–with nothing to offer and only trust to invest. Stop trying and start trusting by releasing your awareness of your inabilities to the God who cares. He loves you just the way you are and sees you as perfect through Christ.

   c. Move past self-awareness and God's forgiveness by sharing your situation with a trusted friend or accountability partner.

   d. You break the most habit strands when you pre-think release, asking God to help you "want to want to" stop any bad behavior. It's like applying superpower to your big fistful of habit strands, and you can break more than you'd imagine possible by engaging in this most simple act of faith. Trust God.

3. **Receive** God's wonderful exchange gift. If you skip this step, your desire for the old habit will continue to drive you toward it.

     a. As you receive God's exchange gifts each time you release any aspect of your habit to Him, you'll find yourself eager to develop the new habit, willing to practice, eager to discover ways to avoid unnecessary temptations, and ready to pre-think ways to respond in cases of unavoidable temptation. These all break additional habit strands.

     b. Even past receiving the original exchange gift, open your heart and mind to any additional input from the Holy Spirit. Each interaction helps.

4. **Respond** by thanking God for His provision and asking Him what you should do next. This part of the process is like submerging all those broken pieces of pasta into the boiling hot water of God's Word. Limp and easy to slide away, they are no longer of any threat to your soul. The hot water also serves to clean the kettle—that's you! You may have gotten a little starchy as the broken pasta cooked in the flow through vessel of your life. If so, the water of God's Word can wash you clean so you are ready to proceed, fast forward, toward your desired new habit.

> The deep roots of our habits tend to surprise us, but God is never surprised.

Marnie Swedberg

The deep roots of our habits tend to surprise us, but God is never surprised. In fact, He knew these habits would tempt us and bring us into captivity before we were even born. In His love, He sent Jesus, rescued us from sin, and provides a simple path out.

In God's economy, the worse your existing habit nightmare, the greater His opportunity to bless you as you yield yourself to Him, one thought at a time, until He becomes your natural breath.

The Beautiful Flow of a Godly Habit

When we factor in God's forgiveness, plus a heaping scoop of God-given patience, habits are neither scary nor difficult to break, just time consuming. We must yield ourselves to the process and celebrate the relational feast we enjoy along the way toward freedom from our bad habits.

In the end, we are developing the most powerful, positive, and pervasively good habit of all: Living a life full of God and letting Him flow His love through ours.

Remember the straw illustration in which the glass is never actually empty? It works both ways! As we release our bad habits, attitudes, worries, or fears to God, the space these consumed in our lives is emptied into His fire of refinement and replaced with the holy breath of His fresh air. Our souls are satisfied, one breath at a time.

> Our souls are satisfied, one sip at a time.

This need for constant air supply from God used to make me crazy. I mean, who has time to sit around praying all the time? Still, His instructions were as clear as could be: Pray without ceasing.

I couldn't figure it out until God taught me the dolphin analogy. Like I always say, "Everything is hard until you know how!"

Upon understanding that I was an earth dweller but a prayer breather, I was able to rest into the beautiful rhythm of breathing God. Up for air, through prayer, back down to business for a few minutes. Repeat. Repeat. Repeat.

Research Confirms God's Method

Psychological research shows that a change of motivation, environment, or relationship can speed habit transformation. God built us this way.

Motivation. This takes us back to the #1 reason habit changes fail: We aren't ready. Maybe we were ready for our first few small changes, but when we hit a step that finds us unprepared for progress, we have to stop because the road is blocked by our lack of motivation.

If you are lacking motivation, go to God. Employ the 4Rs. Recognize that lack. Release the lack and any resulting emotions to God. Receive His exchange gift. Respond with thanks and your offer of availability.

Not always, but often, He has asked me to read about or research information to help me understand why He is asking me to forge forward past the point where I feel ready. What I've learned along the way is that every single change God requests of us is for our own good. He is the most loving parent imaginable, always watching out for our best interests.

When I started the 100-pound weight loss journey I'm still on, I understood only that I was to "enjoy every bite, eating with God." During many of those bites I would pray, "God, teach me how to eat."

I began to be drawn to healthful information sources, and after 18 months, my husband, a sworn meat-eater, decided we should go vegan. This was a shocking request, as I, too, loved meat, cheese, and dairy products.

Incredibly, by that time God had done so much work in my thinking that I was able and ready to say "yes." That's the power of being changed by God in His time and way.

Was it easy? No! Am I perfect at it? No! Will I ever be perfect? Not on earth! But I can

> When did we come to believe that God expects 100% performance outcomes or He gets mad at us?

develop growing habits that move me closer to flow through mastery, and that is what I'm doing. It may be a long, slow process involving a lot of work and conscious choices.

Michael Jordan developed his God-given skills to make him a basketball star. Not content to be an average player, he worked hard. All his effort yielded a measly 49.7% success rate when it came to making baskets during games. With 50% missed shots, he earned a world record.

Read that again: Michael Jordan became one of the world's best basketball players by hitting less than half of the shots he took. He had to be content with that, because it was the best he could do—and better than anyone else in the league at the time.

I like Ty Cobb's baseball world record even better. He holds the record lifetime batting average at just 36.64%, including every single, double, triple, or home run—every hit counted.

I wonder: When did we come to believe that God expects 100% performance outcomes or He gets mad at us?

He created us this way! It's true that in order to get access into His presence and heaven, we must be perfect, but it isn't true that He expects us to attain that level of perfection without Him. He sent Jesus, God in flesh, to pay the price of that requirement because He knew we could never attain it.

In our pride, we think we need to perform and turn in a perfect score or we're in the doghouse with God. I mean, when was the last time you gave yourself a high five for sticking with your new habit less than half of the time?

If you walk away from a bucket of ice cream with one bite uneaten at the bottom, when you would usually have polished off the entire thing, you are making progress! Congratulations! You just realized and released that last bite to God instead of eating it per your usual routine.

You get a point! A pasta noodle breaks. It's a level of success, and God wants to celebrate it with you, not beat you up about the bites you ate.

Now, if you never had the ice cream habit, eating all but a bite of a bucket would not be progress. Once that habit's got hold of you, however, stopping early by a bite, a cup, or a bucketful all count toward your lifetime batting average. You are breaking strongholds, one fistful of pasta at a time.

Define failure as feedback.

In light of the fact that God is a God of relationship and process, simply take the first opportunity to turn your thoughts toward Jesus whenever you become aware of a danger zone. Accept His forgiveness and move toward His love.

Remember, from His perspective, you've already got an "A+."

Environmental Triggers. When you figure out when and where you are exposed to addictive vulnerabilities, employ the 4Rs to ask God what He wants you to do about each. As He prompts ideas to your mind, do whatever He says even if it seems silly or hopeless. Remove things, minimize or eliminate your environmental triggers, walk down a different street, turn off the TV before the infomercials begin, or put a porn blocker on your computer. He may prompt you to make it more difficult to access your trigger foods, drinks, drugs, and so on.

Whenever you are able to change anything for the better, do it. If you switch back, just know you were not quite ready yet. It was a test, and the feedback is valuable.

Define failure as feedback.

It's okay to bat 36.65 or sink 49.7! The missed hits provide useful information. It's a score—nothing more. No need to beat yourself up or get discouraged. Just do what you can, when you can, with Jesus, and call it what it is: progress.

Relational Challenges. It's true some temptations can be eliminated by avoiding the people who trigger or even entice you to engage in your bad habit. Here again, I caution you: Without God in control of your decisions, you may be tempted to take this concept too far.

Years ago, at a website called, ThePerfectLife.com, the owner of the site recommended everyone join him by eliminating all the imperfect relationships in their lives. He'd gotten a divorce from his miserable wife, no longer spoke to his needy mother, and so on. He was on a roll toward the perfect life.

> Only as we accept God's love for us can we extend it to others.

It amused me, in a morbid sort of way, to learn of his sudden death shortly after that post, due to a heart attack.

You see, the trouble with trying to get rid of all the problem people in your life is that you'll eventually have to get rid of yourself, too. You need grace, mercy, and love in your life, just as much as the people around you crave it in theirs.

Only as we accept God's love for us can we extend it to others.

One of the saddest things I see in current counseling is the advice that people divorce in order to more easily move forward in their personal development. I believe this is counterproductive, and I'm sure it breaks God's heart.

Relational challenges sometimes require separation, but more frequently they are boot camps provided for our growth. They can feel like God's act of war on us or the people around us, but again, it's all in the perspective.

Employ the 4Rs to determine what, if any, action you should take. When you are full to overflowing with God's love, you are able to stay in a relationship through even the most difficult circumstances with grace. Let God use every person and problem in your life for His glory.

Let God Flow

Before Jesus died, He shared communion with His disciples explaining that the bread represented His body and the wine His blood. As we contemplate the concept of being a flow through vessel, this analogy becomes even more powerful. Just as blood circulates through the entire body, taking less than 20 seconds for one red blood cell to move through all 60,000 miles of artery, so Jesus, as wine, as spiritual blood, is meant to move freely through us. But we sometimes get in His way.

Bypass surgery is a medical intervention used when fat and plaque block one or more tubes leading to the heart. Abstinence is another type of intervention for times when an addiction is blocking forward progress.

Spiritually, we need God to remove all the junk that clogs His ability to flow through our hearts.

Abstinence is often a necessary step on the way toward freedom, but it is not always God's ultimate goal for you. In fact, if relied upon for life-long habit enforcement, it can be its own habit—a bondage by another name.

God's goal for you is not that you will forever and ever want to go back to your old, default responses, needing abstinence to avoid them, but that you will learn to hate them and never want to use them again. Herein lies freedom.

As an example, when I quit drinking Diet Coke, it was torture. Even though each detoxification experience included headaches, nausea, body aches, and full blown flu-like symptoms, it took me multiple attempts before I could actually be free of the addiction. Now, five years out, when I take a swig of Diet Coke, it tastes like acid. Since I imagine toilet bowl cleaner tasting better than that, why would I ever want to drink it again?

True habit replacement for me was moving from needing 132 ounces a day for decades, to disgust. It's not that I can't have it any more; I can have it anytime I want. It's that I honestly don't want it anymore. I am free of any desire or need to have it.

I was, eventually, able to quit cold turkey, but getting me to that point took years of release.

God's long-term goal for us is that we experience so much transformation that we can no longer even imagine responding to:

- A hurtful word with retaliation.
- Bad news with a mental replay of every other bad thing that has happened to us.
- Pain with self-inflicted intensification.
- Uncertainty with a frenzied search for an instant answer or ultimate hopelessness.
- Thoughts about sins of our past with despair, self-punishment, or amplification.

Instead, a flow through life with God offers you something radically different indeed! After your initial "reactionary thought," (which by the way, is NOT your responsibility,) you will come to enjoy the most amazing habitual responses:

- Hurtful words? Your new default response will kick in, allowing you to invite God to lead you quickly into truth, peace, and a God-honoring reaction.

> A flow through life with God offers you something radically different indeed!

- Bad news? Make your new favorite response this prayer, "Jesus, help me understand this from your perspective." Instantly the light shines into the dark space, and darkness has to leave when a light switch is flipped on. The brilliance of God's presence dispels all darkness, enlightening the mind to how the news is viewed from a heavenly point of view. You will be able to comprehend what is really going on and what to do next.
- Pain? Focusing on God with every breath is the spiritual equivalent of pain relievers. Breathe Jesus until you can pray for advice. Remember: God created your brain to require oxygen for rational thought and your spirit for Him. When you can't think clearly, kick into the "Jesus, Jesus, Jesus" or "God, God, God, God" response until you have the ability to either be with Him in heaven, or get through whatever it is, with Him, here on earth.
- Uncertainty? Never fear! God is near, and He will lead you into a place of peace, until He sheds light on your next steps.
- Thoughts about "sins of your past"? Even if people never forgive you, you can rejoice in the fact that God has. Use these thoughts to remember God's forgiveness, to apply that same forgiveness to yourself, and then to extend it to your tormentors. This is the flow through process that we are talking about.

Section V:

Trust Issues with God

Chapter 10
Identifying God's Presence In Your Past

Your relationship with God often directly mirrors past or present relationships with those in authority over you, like bosses or parents. As you will see from the pyramids that follow, these human relationships may have damaged your prospects with God. You may have automatically transferred some qualities to God that don't truly define Him.

Look at the pyramid chart below. As you begin to think of how your perception of authority figures may be affecting your relationship with God, assess your attitudes toward current or previous bosses.

> You may have automatically transferred some qualities to God that don't truly define Him.

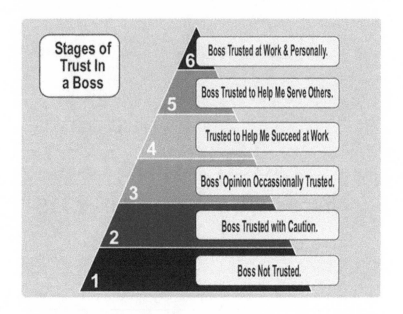

"Why" Questions to Consider

1. At Trust Level 1, why would you keep working for a boss you didn't trust? People have reasons. What are some you can think of?

2. Why would moving to a Trust Level of 2 or 3 still be a big problem at work?

3. Why would you prefer a Trust Level 4 or 5 relationship with your boss? What difference would it make to you and those around you?

4. Why do most employees feel a Trust Level 6 is nearly the impossible dream with a boss? How do you personally feel about this? Do you have first-hand or anecdotal experience to back up your impressions about this? Have you ever seen it work? If so, when? How did it work?

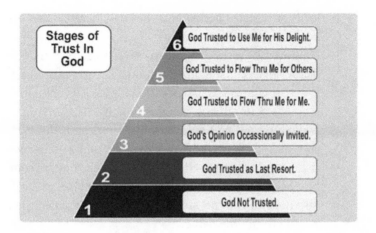

Stages of Trust In God

6 — God Trusted to Use Me for His Delight.

5 — God Trusted to Flow Thru Me for Others.

4 — God Trusted to Flow Thru Me for Me.

3 — God's Opinion Occassionally Invited.

2 — God Trusted as Last Resort.

1 — God Not Trusted.

Our Trust Levels with God

We'll dissect the following pyramid from the bottom up, because the bottom is the default level. We all start at Trust Level 1—we don't trust God! Any upward motion with God is intentional vs. automatic.

1. **No Confidence in God.** This level is often a sheer unawareness of God's existence, who He really is, or that He is available to us personally. This level of distrust in God causes us to reject our need for Him and replace Him with just about anything else. We may find ourselves trusting in the craziest things in order to avoid trusting in God.

2. **Opportunistic Faith.** This level of interaction is almost more affronting than no faith at all. Here we only trust God when we feel we can personally benefit from the transaction. Think of a wayward child who refuses a parent's love, gifts, or help, only calling home when she lands in jail. Even then, she reaches out not because she

loves or respects her parents, but only because they are her last resort. Opportunistic.

3.   **Diplomatic Faith**. This is where we assign God the role of advisor or consultant but retain all power of attorney. We trust Him enough to occasionally ask His opinion or seek His counsel, but we refuse to give Him any rights related to making final decisions. He is basically a no-vote partner in the relationship. We comfort ourselves that we are talking to Him and keeping the lines of communication open, all the while keeping Him at a safe distance from our pet sins and addictions. Independence is still our middle name.

4.   **Testing Faith.** This is where we start realizing God exists for us personally. In Level 4, we begin to trust God with our own small and even medium to large challenges. Like an apprentice electrician testing a light switch he's just installed, we flip our faith up and down, marveling at the resulting light. In this stage we are exploring the fundamentals of how faith in God works. We trust Him now, but mostly because it is in our best interest to do so.

5.   **Sharing Faith.** Once convinced God is for us and not against us, our trust grows. It is during this stage of confidence that we become willing to ask God to extend His help to those we love. Here we are trusting God because it is in the best interest of others.

6.   **Full Confidence.** Upon seeing God's willingness to meet our needs and the needs of our loved ones, we come into an amazing position of trust in Him. Our entire life becomes a reciprocation of gratitude—not to earn His help or favor, but as our only way of saying,

"Thank You" to Him for everything He has done and continues to do for us. As we internalize His goodness and marvel at His personal engagement with us in our everyday lives, we find it the obvious response to yield ourselves completely to His wishes. Finally, we are trusting God for Jesus' sake because He created us for relationship.

What's fascinating is that we may find ourselves at multiple levels simultaneously: Possibly trusting God completely,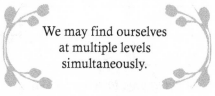

We may find ourselves at multiple levels simultaneously.

at a Level 6, for our eternal salvation while using Him at a Level 4 for everyday crises, and keeping Him at a distant Level 2 as it relates to things we feel we can handle without Him.

Many people who have a deep faith in God have little benefit of Him in their daily lives because they've reserved God's presence, help, and love for only certain circumstances. As for the rest, they automatically try to handle life on their own.

If you trust a doctor with your health, a babysitter with your children, and a contractor with a set of house plans, doesn't it seem fair God would ask you to trust Him with your life?

Trust Level Score Sheet

Using the following table, put today's date in the correct box to identify your current trust level with God for each category. Come back and update your score over time. It will be fun to see growth. (Additional score sheets in Appendix II.)

	Eternity	Health & Future	Money & Bills	Family & Friends	Daily Needs	Small Stuff
No Confidence						
Opportunistic						
Diplomatic						
Testing						
Sharing						
Fully Confident						

The categories to score include:

Eternity   At what level are you trusting God for what happens to you after you die?

Health   At what level are you trusting God to take care of your physical body now and in the future?

Money   At what level are you trusting God in the area of finances?

People   At what level are you trusting God in your relationships?

Daily Needs   At what level are you trusting God to meet your daily needs?

Small Stuff   At what level are you trusting God when you face small challenges like losing your keys or not knowing how to spend the next 15 minutes?

Chapter 11
Possibility Thinking with God

*P*ossibility thinking is threatened when we feel accused or afraid, even with God.

When my kids were little, and even now, when I manage employees, I often ask the question, "Why do you think I asked you to do it like that?"

A mature response kicks in with possibility thinking, seeking to identify my reasons for requesting something to be done in a particular way. Conversely, an immature, reactionary response, usually comes back in some variation of, "Because you said so," or, "Because you're the boss."

This chapter exists to help you get past all the automatic, self-defense responses you have come to call normal as they relate to your spiritual habits of experiencing God. My goal is to help you move into possibility thinking about why you might like to start trusting God more from this moment forward.

God Wrote the Bible for You

Do you remember how God created time for you? God also wrote a love letter to you.

The Bible is a compilation of three-quarter million words, 31,000 verses, 1,100 chapters, and 66 books that God flowed through men, to help you understand His love and provision for you.

The entire Bible, from beginning to end, tells one consistent story: God created man; man rejected God; God sent His Son, Jesus Christ, to pay the penalty for that rejection; Jesus lived, died, and rose again, ascending into heaven where He now intercedes for us.

I've come to love exploring the reasons "why" behind everything. As a mentor, I often challenge

> I have found Him to be everything He claims to be: Holy God, wholly good.

my mentees to dig down to the fifth or sixth level of "why" answers before encouraging them to move forward toward any proposed shift.

The habit of shutting down "why" questions jeopardizes our ability to think creatively, locking us into historical, experience-based thinking.

Let's look for some proof why the Bible might actually be God's love letter to you. It was written by eyewitnesses with compelling evidence to win the case:

- Over a 1,600 year span,
- In three languages,
- On three continents,
- In locations from deserts to dungeons, and palaces to prisons,

- In times of war and peace, poverty and prosperity,
- By over 40 authors in positions from prophets to peasants, and kings to tax collectors.

No committee you have ever been on has been able to agree about everything. Even ten skilled surgeons, working at one medical facility, discussing the course of action for one complex patient scenario, can never fully agree about anything. Yet, the entire Bible does! It is from God, told in story form, and He transferred it, via His flow through vessels back then, for our benefit now.

In addition, the Bible contains over 2500 prophecies, 2000 of which have already been fulfilled without error. The scientific likelihood of this "just happening" is near impossible.

As further evidence, I would like to take the witness stand myself to tell you what Jesus means to me. It's my testimony, my personal experience with God.

Jesus Christ was introduced to me when I was a child as the One who created me, loves me, and longs to have a relationship with me. I accepted Him, as my sin-substitute, when I was just four years old. It was memorable and life-changing. The only other things I remember as vividly at age four were extremely traumatic events. But, on the day I met Jesus, I can tell you where I was, how I felt, and how my feelings changed after meeting God.

I have loved Him ever since. Not perfectly, but I have loved and trusted this God. I have found Him to be everything He claims to be: Holy God, wholly good.

He is my Savior and Lord. He has personally shepherded me through devastating events that would have otherwise left me broken, relationally ruined, financially destitute, or dead.

I am here to testify He is not simply an opinion or historical fact; He is God. He is Truth and He is my life. My greatest goal, my highest aim, is to yield every last bit of myself to Him as His flow through vessel while I am here on earth, and then go spend eternity with Him in heaven.

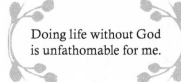

Doing life without God is unfathomable for me.

Doing life without God is unfathomable for me. It is outside my realm of possibilities to try to think of living one day without God.

Why Questions Work

As you go forward in your life, make it a new habit to switch out every accusatory "why" with a creative "why":

- Instead of, "Why did God do this to me?" Ask, "Daddy, why did you allow this into my life?" I cannot even begin to tell you how many times this sincere question has turned a potential disaster into a blessing within minutes, days, or months.
- Instead of a hopeless, whining, "Why me?" send up a playful response like "Why does it get to be me again?" Your love and adoration for what God's about to do for, in, or through you demonstrates your faith in Him.
- Instead of, "Why not me?" ask a humble question to Your loving Father, "Daddy, since You know I really wanted that, why didn't You give it to me?" It's amazing how vulnerable God makes Himself when we are truly interested in how He makes decisions.

I have had some of the most profound insights upon asking questions in a humble way after grievous disappointments. God is not obligated to explain Himself, but He often chooses to do so. If not now, then over time.

Marnie Swedberg

Self Test: Trusting God

The goal of this section is to engage your brain into possibility thinking: What if you were to consider moving your faith in God up a notch?

I have added some answers to get you started, but be sure to add your own "whys" in each category. Remember, your early life experiences may have preprogrammed you to hear all these "why" questions as accusatory, when they are actually powerfully positive.

To the best of your ability, relax and trust that God fully understands that you have simply been doing your best up to this point in your life. As you work through this exercise, open your heart to Him. Let Him heal you of all that has gone before and usher you into a new and vibrant life with Him.

Answer these questions in your own way:

- Why would God ask you to trust Him? A few possibilities include:
    - ❏ He is insecure and needs validation.
    - ❏ He actually thinks He's God.
    - ❏ He enjoys bossing people around.
    - ❏ He gets a thrill out of the feeling of power He wields.
    - ❏ He is aware of rules/laws that make things work better.
    - ❏ He loves us and has the power to actually change outcomes.
    - ❏ Write your own ideas:

- What are some reasons you've heard for refusing to believe in God?
    - ❏ Don't believe there is a God.
    - ❏ Don't believe God is as good as He says He is.
    - ❏ Don't believe God can be accessed by humans.

- ❑ Don't believe God cares.
- ❑ Have tried to trust God, but were disappointed.
- ❑ Have trusted God and found God wanting.
- ❑ Feel trusting God would require accountability and possibly even obedience to things you're unwilling to do.
- ❑ Write your own ideas:

- Why would someone trust God as a last resort?
    - ❑ Precisely because He is their last resort. Anytime sooner would seem unreasonable to them.
    - ❑ There is a flicker of hope that God might care. This feeling is enough for desperate times, but not enough to actually apply to everyday situations.
    - ❑ Write your own ideas:

- Why would God honor a last resort prayer?
    - ❑ He actually cares.
    - ❑ He's the one that caused the trouble in the first place in order to force the person to recognize His availability.
    - ❑ He is gracious, receiving even the smallest token of faith as a gesture of good will in His direction.
    - ❑ Write your own ideas:

- Why would someone use God as a consultant?
    - ❑ He just might be able to help.
    - ❑ In hopes His advice will line up with their wishes and trump the other input standing in the way of progress.
    - ❑ He's the perfect consultant! He sees the big picture.
    - ❑ He's a great One to have on your team. He's got power and pull.
    - ❑ Just having Him around gives you a sense of security.
    - ❑ Write your own ideas:

- Why would God ever serve in the capacity of a consultant?
  - ❑ He's used to it. His book, the Bible, is used in that way every day.
  - ❑ He knows some input is better than none.
  - ❑ His goal is to eventually gain more of your trust and He sees the value in letting you move gradually in His direction.
  - ❑ Write your own ideas:

- Why would God want to live through the life of a human?
  - ❑ He loves us and knows life with Him is far superior to life without Him.
  - ❑ He values our personalities and how His character flowing through our lives makes them the best they can be.
  - ❑ He created us to need Him. Flowing through us was always the plan.
  - ❑ The reality of an abundant life requires an endless source of power, and He's got plenty of power to share.
  - ❑ Write your own ideas:

- Why would anyone trust God to take over their life?
  - ❑ No sane person would.
  - ❑ He created us. He'd know best how to maximize the design.
  - ❑ He is God. Who better to trust?
  - ❑ Life is tough. We could use some help!
  - ❑ Write your own ideas:

- Why would God use one person to bless another?
  - ❑ The other person is incapable of asking on their own behalf.
  - ❑ The other person doesn't know about God yet.
  - ❑ The other person's faith is small or misguided.

❏ He uses the opportunity to bless both the helper and the person being helped.

❏ Write your own ideas:

- Why would anyone use their own relationship with God for the benefit of someone else?

  ❏ Giving is one of the most rewarding experiences of life.

  ❏ If you have enough to spare, you can easily share.

  ❏ Watching someone else in pain is sometimes harder than bearing the pain ourselves.

  ❏ When we've experienced something superior, we want others to experience it, too.

  ❏ We know God has enough to share with everyone. His love and ability to be involved is unlimited. There is no fear it will run out if we share it.

  ❏ Write your own ideas:

- Why would God find pleasure in a human wholly devoted to Him?

  ❏ As creator, He loves to see His creation used for its intended purposes and to its fullest capacity.

  ❏ As a parent, each child is unique and special, loved for himself in his own way. God is the Ultimate Parent.

  ❏ As a helper, there's no better place to live than inside a person, always ready at hand to assist and aid.

  ❏ As a deity, being praised is part of His character. Receiving praise willingly offered, without coercion, is the best kind.

  ❏ Write your own ideas:

- Why would I ever let God use me for His own purposes?

  ❏ I've counted the cost and can't think of anything that would have a higher return on investment than yielding everything I am to God.

Marnie Swedberg

❏ There's no safer place to be than in God's care.
❏ Regardless of circumstances, I always get to be with God, with instant access to Him at all times.
❏ Write your own ideas:

God Really Loves You

Imagine for a moment that God really loves you.

- If God was a human parent, He would train you so you could succeed in life.
- If He was an architect, He would add hidden features only He knew about.
- If He was an embroiderer, He would create amazing scenes for the public view while not worrying about the messy threads on the backside.
- If He was an orchestra conductor, He would delight in the harmonies as much as in scheduled dissonance.
- If He was playwright, He would build drama into the script so things wouldn't get boring.
- If He was a chef, He would spice things up in an unlimited number of ways for new adventures everyday.

As the Captain of your personal boat ride through life, God journeys with you from start to finish. He extends to you a lovely, first class cabin, or a cot in the Captain's cabin.

Stay near the Captain.

He allows you to choose from limitless excursions, concerts, magic shows, and more, all for your cruising entertainment. You may go where He goes, sit at His table, and hang out with His friends, or not.

Get on this ship, my friend. Stay near the Captain. Room with Him and select only the expeditions He suggests and is willing to chaperon. Get to know His people and enjoy the ride.

Sure, there are going to be storms at sea, maybe even some hurricanes, but He's got it all under control. He will bring you safely to your desired haven.

Godly Wealth Roster

One of the hardest things to accept is a "no" or "later" answer from God. Especially when situations seem desperate, not receiving an answer to prayer in a timely manner can crush our faith in God. But, God has reasons for every decision—good, good reasons.

A few years ago I hosted the Godly Wealth Expo to clearly explain God's perspective on wealth. My guests were Andy Robbins, Dr. Nick Castellano and Brian Kluth. Andy took us through biblical proof of God's intent to bless us at every opportunity. Nick shared stories of how God gifted him with millions of dollars, back-to-back, to prove His blessing and next-step directions for Nick. Brian shared how God had called him to live on a salary of $1 per year, trusting God alone for everything his family needed. Each guest made a compelling case for God's love, goodness, provision, and desire to bless us in every way possible while accomplishing His work on earth.

I encourage you to listen to the archived recordings free of charge at www.GodlyWealthExpo.com and below find a small version of the 8.5 x 11 inch rendition of the "Godly Wealth Roster" I created to help us visualize the complexity of God's decision-making process.

You write your request on the left side, then circle any code letters you feel would be affected by a Yes/Now answer or conversely a Later/No answer. Leave the outcomes column blank until you see how God answers. I've found that frequently the Later/No answers provide far more character growth potential than the Yes/Now answer I'd prefer in the moment.

Use the chart to increase your faith in the God who knows you best, loves you most, and is committed to your conformity to the image of Christ.

Additional blank worksheets in Appendix II.

Godly Wealth Analysis	Results if Answer Is:	Results if Answer Is:	What You See Now
Need, Request, Vision, Dream	Yes / Now	Later / No	Outcomes
	$ C D F G H I J K L N P S T U V W Y	$ C D F G H I J K L N P S T U V W Y	
	$ C D F G H I J K L N P S T U V W Y	$ C D F G H I J K L N P S T U V W Y	
	$ C D F G H I J K L N P S T U V W Y	$ C D F G H I J K L N P S T U V W Y	
	$ C D F G H I J K L N P S T U V W Y	$ C D F G H I J K L N P S T U V W Y	
	$ C D F G H I J K L N P S T U V W Y	$ C D F G H I J K L N P S T U V W Y	
	$ C D F G H I J K L N P S T U V W Y	$ C D F G H I J K L N P S T U V W Y	
	$ C D F G H I J K L N P S T U V W Y	$ C D F G H I J K L N P S T U V W Y	
	$ C D F G H I J K L N P S T U V W Y	$ C D F G H I J K L N P S T U V W Y	
	$ C D F G H I J K L N P S T U V W Y	$ C D F G H I J K L N P S T U V W Y	
	$ C D F G H I J K L N P S T U V W Y	$ C D F G H I J K L N P S T U V W Y	
	$ C D F G H I J K L N P S T U V W Y	$ C D F G H I J K L N P S T U V W Y	

How to Use this Chart:
1. Enter something you want from God.
2. Circle benefits of a "Yes" or "Now" answer.
3. Circle the benefits of "Later" or "No."
4. Present your request with an open hand.
5. Enter the outcome asap when it's obvious.

$ Generosity
C Contentment
D Diligence
F Faithfulness
G Goodness
H Humility
I Kindness
J Joy
K Knowledge
L Love

Gentleness
Peace
Self-Control
Patience
Purity
Forgiveness
Wisdom
Honesty

N
P
S
T
U
V
W
Y

Also remember: Timing.
ie - Christmas/Bday Gifts are held for a particular day. Babies, plants, etc., have specific gestation periods.

Section VI

Epilogue

Chapter 12
The Rest of Your Story

*I*n order for you to fully trust God with your life here, you need to fully trust Him with your eternity. You already know how I feel about cartoons that make heaven look silly, but there is one exception—a heaven joke I really do love. I don't know whom to credit as I heard it from a friend and it's included on numerous online joke sites. It's about a rich man who died and was met by Saint Peter at the pearly gates.

Peter asked for his name and then said inquisitively, "You brought a suitcase?"

The rich man replied, "Yep! I asked God about it in advance, and He said it would be OK."

Peter, curious, leaned forward and opened the bag. With a grin threatening to erupt into hilarity, Peter looked up from the pile of gold bullion and said, "You brought pavement?!"

Heaven is amazing!

Heaven is amazing! We will be together with God, face to face, forever! It is beyond our comprehension in the best way possible.

Time Will Be No More

One of my favorite aspects of heaven is its timelessness. If you know me at all, you know I am busy! I write, but I also manage our local family restaurant and retail store,

> ...with God,
> face to face.

host an online ministry and weekly radio talk show, do media, and speak at live events; plus I'm a wife, mom, daughter, sister and friend.

I find comfort in the fact that time is different with God. He says, "One day is like a thousand years and a thousand years is like a day." Talk about superlatives!

We also know God is all-present, regardless of time and space. He took John, the author of Revelations, on a tour to see the end of the world. John wrote down what he saw, to the best of his ability. I love it! He saw huge flying grasshoppers, our modern day helicopters. He saw so many things he could barely describe, but we can understand them now. Incredible!

> Heaven is going to be
> one long, never-ending,
> "The Rest of the Story."

I am especially fond of books and movies based on real life stories. I think God is the biggest fan of a great story. The Bible is basically a giant story book for our benefit. I think heaven is going to be one long, never-ending, "The Rest of the Story." Time will be no object and we'll get to experience every full-length version we could ever be interested in viewing.

There's More to Every Story

Have you ever had someone thank you for doing something for them in the past that didn't even hit your radar? It was so small to you, so insignificant, that you could hardly remember doing it, let alone would you expect thanks for it at this later date.

These moments of surprise gratitude here on earth should remind us that the best is yet to come. When we get to heaven, people will be coming up to us and sharing how our small, flow through actions, changed their trajectory.

It is the Divine opposite of the New Zealand aircraft crash in 1979, which killed all 257 people aboard. The plane was programmed just two degrees off course. The pilots were not aware of this mistake and flew into the side of a 12,000 foot mountain. The two-degree coordinate difference placed them 28 miles east of where they thought they were, and due to cloud cover, they could not see to avoid the crash.

We have the opportunity to serve as God's two-degree course correctors often without even knowing it.

When we allow God to flow through us, He takes seemingly insignificant encounters and transforms them into massive benefit, both here and in eternity. He also provides direct and powerful assistance anytime we cry out for help, so we never have to worry we'll run out or won't be able to help "enough."

Do you know that feeling you have while watching a good movie you know has a happy ending? I believe there will be time, opportunity, and the ability to replay all of life's stories with none of their emotional drain. We'll be able to settle in for one amazing story-ride after another, all from the safety of our heavenly home.

In fact, I believe my dad and others who have gone before are actually watching our lives

> We have the opportunity to serve as God's two-degree course correctors often without even knowing it.

with that level of comfort and confidence right now. What seems to us as an endless series of falls and failures, or terrible trials, to them appear in their reality: One more stepping stone on our path toward heaven.

Heaven's Secret Surprise

Having lived and journeyed through so many traumas myself and with others, I have come to believe the number one thing that will surprise us when we get to heaven is God's timing.

I sometimes imagine myself in God's shoes, just to try to gain some perspective:

- God is coordinating everything on earth, in the universe, and in heaven. I think He likes the challenge. I know I like a challenge! I like to coordinate plans for myself, my leadership team, my staff, my family, and others. It's a lot of work, and it's tough due to all the moving pieces, but it can be fun.
- God is scheduling all of time, from beginning to end, meeting prophesied deadlines, right on time. I schedule staff for our businesses. It takes me hours every month to get it right. There are so many moving pieces. Just imagine what God's got going on!
- God has invited us to a giant banquet He's planning for our arrival in heaven. Here on earth, He's coordinating all the travel, housing, and meal arrangements for the trip up, so we have the best ride possible on the way. I have hosted parties for over 1000 and have coordinated events in multiple cities all at once, but I can't fathom the event planning mastery required to do His job.

Managing the world and bringing us in for a landing, right on time, is no easy flight, even for an experienced pilot like God.

Marnie Swedberg

Throw in the mind-numbing factor of giving billions of people free will, and you've got yourself a serious challenge!

But God... I love that phrase and I say it all the time.

But God is the Master Planner with all power, and He is going to bring the world to its prophesied end, while allowing each human to choose their own eternal destiny.

But God...
I love that phrase.

He even allows us to retain our will after we choose to trust Him, making it an ongoing choice to partner with Him or not, within the benefits of that original agreement.

A Favorite Motto

I have a lot of mottos. I suppose I'm most famous for this one: "There is time to do everything God wants me to do!"

I always follow up by explaining that there is not time to do everything—there is not time to do everything good, there is not time to do everything everyone else wants me to do, and there's not even time to do everything I want to do. But if God is God, then there must be time to do everything He wants me to do.

I've included many more mottos and prayer phrases in my book, *Feeling Loved: Connecting with God in the Minutes You Have*. The one I'll share in a moment is about trusting God when the timing of things doesn't make any sense.

Waiting can be torture! Perspective can be gained if you think about Christmas. What loving parent would allow their children to open all their gifts before Christmas? No matter how much begging, pleading, or bargaining ensues, a healthy parent, one who does not need instant gratification or external validation from their offspring, simply refuses to ruin the effect of Christmas by giving in to childish pleas.

The wonder of Christmas is well worth the wait: It is gift heaped upon gift, reserved for a certain time, in celebration of the greatest gift ever given, Jesus Christ—the Christ of Christmas.

Like children being "tortured" with the wait, we face continual, often painful, and frequently incomprehensible waits that torment us and threaten to shipwreck our faith in God.

Several years ago, after seeing God come through in a situation that looked utterly impossible, I adopted this catch-phrase which I love to say in times of confusion:

"I choose to be as thankful in this moment as I will be when I meet Jesus face-to-face and understand everything He is doing right now to help me, protect me, and provide for me."

I know in that moment I will comprehend everything and will be utterly ashamed for any lack of faith, or if I get it right now, be laughing out loud or crying tears of joy with God as He unfolds the gifts He's been waiting to reveal. I want to choose faith every single time!

> I want to choose faith every single time!

God Heals His Way

Our faith to wait on God is most severely tested when it comes to sitting near the sick bed of someone we love. We recall that God called the disciples "perverse" when they couldn't heal the little boy, so we feel frustrated when God doesn't respond to our pleas for healing, even when we invest the most faith we can muster in our heartfelt requests to this Almighty God.

Since the earliest records of man (found in the Bible), people have experienced healing via numerous methods including:

1. Self-Directed.
2. Doctor-Driven.

3. Sleep-Induced.
4. Miraculous.

The question of faith mostly addresses the fourth type of healing, but to do it justice, we must spend a moment understanding the first three types.

Self-Directed Healing. Throughout our lives, we experience numerous illnesses and injuries for which a natural process of healing exists. A virus is cured with time, rest, and fluids, while a cut is cured when we clean and cover it.

Doctor-Driven Healing. Some illnesses and injuries are beyond the scope of home remedies, at which point we seek the help of a trained physician. Doctors are among God's many gifts to us for healing.

Sleep-Induced Healing. Some illnesses are intended by God to lead to death at which point healing comes as the saint "falls asleep" and awakens in heaven, where there is no more sickness and no more tears. This, too, is a gift for the believer.

Miraculous Healing. When healing is elusive and death does not come, we are stuck to endure the ravages of the pain. It is at these times that even non-God-honoring people seek supernatural intervention.

As a flow through vessel for God, you may be asked to pray with someone for healing, and if so, you need to understand God's methods for answering such a prayer.

The Bible provides many examples of healing, more than 40 in Jesus' ministry alone. There is a pattern that emerges, and understanding it will help you pray with "all faith" for healing, anytime you are asked to do so.

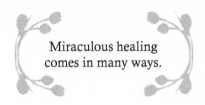

Miraculous healing comes in many ways.

Miraculous healing comes in many ways. Below we will look at the stories of four blind men, healed by the same Healer, but with three unique styles or methods.

1. **Instant and Complete Healing**. As recorded in both Luke 18 and Matthew 9, blind men asked for healing and Jesus simply gave it to them. In one moment, they went from blind to full, perfect vision. Instant healing is the kind we all want! We want it so badly that we often ignore or undervalue any other type.

2. **Gradual Healing**. In Mark 8, Jesus used a process. First, He took the blind man's hand and led him out of the city, then spit on his eyes, asked for a progress report, and learned the man was partially healed, so put His hands on his eyes. Then the man was healed.

    Sometimes there are multiple steps and/or touch points. In this example, the healing occurred within a few minutes, but I've seen examples where the miraculous healing occurred over the course of years. Nevertheless, a blind-man-seeing *is* miraculous, no matter how long it takes.

3. **Healing Requiring Personal Action**. In John 9, Jesus spat on the ground and made clay, which He put on the man's eyes. Next, He sent the man to wash in the pool of Siloam. Upon completing this task, his sight was restored.

God alone determines when, who, and how to heal. Having the faith to ask Him is our part, but deciding how He will comply is His part. Use the 4Rs, as always, to understand your part.

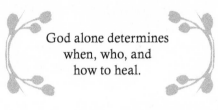

God alone determines when, who, and how to heal.

Recognize healing is needed and God is able.

Release your preconceived ideas, desperate feelings, and the need to Him.

Receive His choice of exchange gifts for you (often peace, patience, hope, or comfort).

Respond with a "Thank You" and a willingness to assist.

There is one additional healing pattern that is critical to understand before you launch any type of healing ministry.

Earthly Limitations

Most days the eyewitness accounts report Jesus healing "all" who came to Him. Yet, at the Pool of Bethesda, He chose just one man to heal while leaving the rest of the invalids lying in their pain and helplessness.

We are simply God's conduits.

Only upon our arrival in heaven will we understand how hard that had to be for Jesus, and the level of obedience it required. His disciples, too, must have wondered why, with infinite healing power, He simply walked away from the other needy people without healing them that day.

When praying for miraculous healing, it is important for us
to remember which of us is God: It's not me! It's not you. It's not
the person requesting prayer.

We are simply God's conduits. He never got angry at the disciples for lacking the skill to heal; He was frustrated with them
because they failed to allow God's power to flow through them.
They had missed opportunities to develop their faith muscles,
through prayer and fasting, so when the critical moment arrived,
they could not further God's kingdom because their faith was
too small.

In His most famous sermon, Jesus listed nine things as blessings that we might label curses:

1. Blessed are the poor in spirit, for theirs is the kingdom
    of heaven.
2. Blessed are those who mourn, for they shall be
    comforted.
3. Blessed are the meek, for they shall inherit the earth.
4. Blessed are those who hunger and thirst for righteous-
    ness, for they shall be filled.
5. Blessed are the merciful, for they shall obtain mercy.
6. Blessed are the pure in heart, for they shall see God.
7. Blessed are the peacemakers, for they shall be called
    sons of God.
8. Blessed are those who are persecuted for righteousness'
    sake, for theirs is the kingdom of heaven.
9. Blessed are you when they revile and persecute
    you, and say all kinds of evil against you falsely for
    My sake.

He went on to say, "Rejoice and be exceedingly glad, for great
is your reward in heaven." (Matthew 5)

Marnie Swedberg

As we approach the throne of grace from this position of submission, joy, faith, and humility, we remove every hindrance which could prevent God from providing for us what He deems best.

Considering He has all of the facts about every situation—past, present, and future—and is **What the godless must call a coincidence, a Christian is invited to call God-incidence.** 100% aware of the potential ramifications and ripple effects of every option, we would be wise to take this Physician's word as final.

Start a Journal

I believe journaling was God's idea first: The Bible is mostly one big, inspired journal highlighting God's faithfulness to mankind.

There is one type of journal I hope you'll start. There's no need to worry about doing it every day or at any precise interval. Just, when you have a prayer request, write the date in the left column, and the request in the middle, leaving a few spaces before your next entry.

At times, I add requests every day for weeks. Other times I don't add anything for months. It is not a requirement, but when I do it, it is incredibly faith-boosting!

What the godless must call a coincidence, a Christian is invited to call God-incidence. Many a God-lover is familiar with a comment similar to this from their non-Christian friends, "You sure have a lot of amazing coincidences in your life!"

At moments like these, we recognize an open door of opportunity and ask permission to share our personal testimony.

Like a witness in a courtroom taking the stand, we share what God has done for us with the goal of convincing the jury (the thoughts in their head) that God is real. We long, more than anything else, that they, too, may know His loving presence, power, and provision in their lives.

Back to the journal, as you enter your requests, be sure to release them to God using the 4Rs. Write down the exchange gift He extends to your heart in that moment. Write a small thank you as you receive the exchange gift and another one later, after you see Him answer each prayer.

My journal has hundreds of "Thank You" notations (TYs) next to answered prayers. When a page has no more pending requests, I place a "TY" in the top right corner. This page need not be reviewed anymore except for pleasure. All prayers have been answered with a "yes" or a "no." Either way, I'm OK and grateful.

Some pages have had the same unanswered prayer for years and years. If this ever discourages me, I give it to God again, reapplying the 4Rs to determine if there is anything else He wants me to do. Often, He gifts me with an exchange thought that renews my faith. All of a sudden I seem to remember how He came through for:

- Abraham, who was promised a son, but had to wait until he was over 90 years old to get Isaac.
- David, who was anointed king as a teenager, but did not get to sit on the throne for over 10 years. Between times, he wandered in the desert with robbers and thieves, and once he even had to act crazy just to save his life. Talk about confusing!
- Daniel, a super-saint being fully obedient to God, was thrown into a lion's den to be torn to shreds. I have had some tough waits in my life, but I've never been taken into captivity, held hostage, or required to spend a night with hungry lions.

Marnie Swedberg

God's plans are perfect, but they often look perplexing and involve pain. Still, reminiscent of the artist who sketches a simple picture and then surprises us by turning it upside down to reveal the real, more impressive drawing, God is the Master of all things.

> God's plans are perfect, but they often look perplexing and involve pain.

When praying the Lord's Prayer before I rise each day, I love it all, but here I'll share how I think about the phrase, "which art in heaven." Four simple, yet profoundly comforting words.

I usually say something like, "Good morning, Daddy! I am so happy that You are up in heaven today with perfect perspective so You can help me while I am down here seeing only what's smack dab in front of my face."

God never promised to explain everything to us. He doesn't have to make sense to us, or more specifically, to our reasoning minds. Neither will He spoil a surprise or reveal His game plan until the perfect time.

What He does ask is for our trust. He then hopes we'll enjoy the ride to the best of our ability, safe in His loving care.

Your Future as a Flow Through Vessel

Life is full of joys and challenges. We have only just begun and, yes, the best is yet to come!

This chapter is full of ideas for your future development. Like a kid in a candy store, you may feel overwhelmed by all you've read in this book. Don't worry! Just pick one concept to start with and go forward with God.

I asked a bunch of godly girl friends to share a crisis response with me and below are a few. I included their names to help

What He does ask
is for our trust.

you internalize the reality that women, just like you, turn to God for hope and help through every situation.

The first time you read the lists below, just highlight any or all that "feel right" to you, then select the "one" that seems best now and start by memorizing, practicing, and using it.

You can always add to your repertoire at any time by picking another or creating your own.

Oh, and by the way, several of these gals submitted a bunch, and most of them included one or more Scripture verses. I chose to include only these because each, even if not a direct quote from the Bible, is based on God's truth. Enjoy!

Easy to Remember Acronyms

The 4Rs = **R**ecognize, **R**elease, **R**eceive, **R**espond. Marnie

P.I.P. = **P**ut **I**t **I**n **P**erspective. Kim Larson

S.P.A. = **S**top! **P**ray! **A**pply! Gaye Lindfors

Q.T.I.P. = **Q**uit **T**aking **I**t **P**ersonally. Carolyn J. Gage

R.E.V. = **R**ecognize negative emotions, **E**valuate thinking & **V**isualize God's truth. Tami Myer

P.R.A.Y. = **P**raise, **R**equest, **A**sk, **Y**ield. Verna Bowman

Short, Meaningful Phrases

"God, Help!"   *Many godly girls*

"Focus on TRUTH instead of the trial."   *Tamra Myrick*

"God, I could use a little help right now."   *Deb Watson*

"It came to pass—not to stay."   *Alice Spenst*

"In acceptance lies peace."   *Barbara Smith*

"Fear is useless. What is needed is trust."   *Deb Scott*

"Stop! Drop! And pray!"   *Marnie*

"I'll pass on that, Satan!"   *Verna LeRay Warner*

"I trust you completely, Lord."   *Brenda Kilber*

"Jesus, Jesus, Jesus" or "God, God, God, God"
                                  Marnie & many godly girls

"Lord, I know this has not caught you by surprise."
                                        Mindy Ferguson

"Jesus, my Guard and Defender, please answer the door."
                                        Sherry Carter

"Bitterness = Bondage." Repeat, repeat, repeat.
                                        Carole Brumley.

"God knew this was going to happen. I know He's got
me covered."   *Glenda Thomas*

"I am loved, and God will work this for good. God is
FOR me!"   *Michelle Maxwell*

"Jesus is my joy, my life, and my all. Jesus is my strength
and my rock."   *Rosie Rygh*

"Let your faith be bigger than your fears because your God
is bigger than anything you're afraid of."
                                        Merindy Morganson

Scripture Crisis Responses You'll Love

Obviously, the Bible is full of great verses for us to love. Spend the rest of your life finding, highlighting, memorizing, and sharing them. To get you going, here's a list of godly girl favorites.

Psalms 91:1	"He that dwelleth in the secret place of the Most High shall abide under the shadow of the Almighty. I will say of the Lord, He is my refuge and my fortress, my God, in Him will I trust." Marnie
Psalms 46:1	"You (Lord) are a very present help in times of need." Forshia Ross
1 John 4:4	"Greater is HE that is in me, than he that is in the world." Many godly girls
I Timothy 1:7	"God has not given us a spirit of fear." Kim Ramiller
II Timothy 1:17	"Be strong and courageous!" Joan Berntson
James 4:7	"Submit to God, resist the devil. Come near to God." Mary Daniels
Romans 8:26	"The Spirit helps us in our weakness." Katy Harms
Romans 8:28	"God works all things for the good of those who love Him." Karen Holmberg-Smith
Mark 5:36	"Be not afraid any longer—only BELIEVE." Nancy Fisher
Hebrews 13:5	"Never will I leave you; never will I forsake you." Carol Krahn
Prov. 18:10	"The name of the Lord is a strong tower." Susan Helweg

Marnie Swedberg

Prov. 3:5-6	"Trust in the Lord with all your heart and lean not on your own understanding. In all your ways, acknowledge Him, and He will direct your paths." Many godly girls
Psalms 46:10	"Be still and know that I Am God!" Many godly girls

Lighthearted Go-To Phrases

Remember how, when I get to the fourth R, respond, I often tease God about His *huge* new problem that I just gave Him? Playfully, I inquire if He feels able to handle *this one*.

When you become proficient at trusting God and rushing to Him for help in every crisis, you will find you often can move from hysteria to humor, or from panic to playful, very quickly.

Below are some godly girl favorite trauma responses that move them directly from fear to faith in one short, humorous phrase.

"I know nothing!"   *Marnie, based on James 4:14a*

"Choosin' joy!"   *Pam Farrel*

"Keep your nose and your toes pointed to Jesus."
                    Erin Campbell

"Jesus, please answer the door."
                    Sherry Carter, when bad thoughts bombard

"Don't wrestle with a pig, you will just get muddy and the pig will love it!"   *Carole Leathem, when wanting to say something unbecoming in response.*

God Will Gift You With Your Own Go-To Phrases

A phrase alone is useless, just like faith in false evidence leads to an unjust verdict. Faith is only as good as the source upon which it relies, and phrases are only as useful as the truth they portray.

After you've walked with God for a season or more, and you have practiced, studied, and learned from His Word, and from those who have gone before you on this journey, you will find yourself embracing new go-to phrases.

Discovering your own analogies and personalized go-tos are just a few of the ways God plays with us, His children. He loves to delight us, share secrets with us, give us opportunities to experience and then flow His love through to others, and provide us with supernatural peace and joy amidst the most audacious abuses, all as part of His plan.

He loves to delight us.

It's Time to Celebrate!

Before I close this book, I encourage you to ponder one last analogy.

Envision Jesus Christ, kneeling in front of you, extending a beautiful engagement ring in your direction. As He asks for your hand in marriage, He has tears in his eyes because He loves you so much. His love led Him to the cross and now He longs for you to accept His invitation to be His bride.

The analogy is profound:

- We are invited to marry a prince whose home is heaven.
- He can marry us all, because to Him, we collectively make up the church: His one bride.
- He can be madly in love with each of us in the same way

a mother can love all her children, finding unique joy and pleasure in each.

I'm dying to know! Have you said yes to Jesus Christ yet? This Bridegroom wants to love and cherish you forever—not only until death do you part, but forever.

If you haven't said "yes" yet, do it now! God extends this offer for only so long: If you die without accepting Jesus as your personal Savior from hell, you will go there—alone and apart from God for the rest of eternity. That's your final answer.

People have told me they could never trust a God who could create a place like hell. If it helps, I don't believe God created hell. I think hell is any space where God is not present.

When people say their lives feel like hell on earth, I believe they are alluding to this absence of God: Hell is where God isn't. Because God is present in believers throughout the world, the world enjoys a measure of goodness, so even if your own life has been vacant of God's presence up until this point, you've only tasted a tiny bit of what hell is like.

Heaven and hell are both superlatives we cannot fathom: Heaven is pure good. Hell is pure evil.

Amazingly, once we accept Christ's proposal, His love covers all our sin. He lavishes His attention, love, and affection on us and we are prepared from that moment

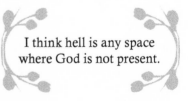

I think hell is any space where God is not present.

forward to marry into the most royal of families. Heaven is our future home, but here in our earthly bodies, in the land of our human birth, we can expect everything we've experienced so far, except with the awareness that we are leaving soon. We'll still experience sickness, disease, pain, separation, tears and more, despite our pleas for our Lover to come rescue us sooner.

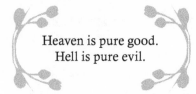

**Heaven is pure good.
Hell is pure evil.**

As we move gradually toward the marriage feast God's planning for us, let's extend to Him at least as much love and patience as we'd offer a human lover. Let's go out of our way to make His day; support His sometimes confusing or insane-looking ideas, convinced they are better than Einstein's; play along with his silly antics, laughing with Him instead of mocking Him; and free up our schedules as much as possible to be available whenever He calls.

It's all a choice: We can live with or without God, filled to overflowing with His love or dependent on our own, part of His-story or busy with our own little lives.

Life Application
Study Guide

Chapter 1. How to Live Beyond Human Limitations

1. In this chapter, I mentioned my habit, "To think of you is
   to pray for you." What is your habitual reaction to thoughts
   of worry? Read Philippians 4:6-7 in your Bible and then
   paraphrase them into your own words below.

2. I have often felt "crazy" when responding to a prompting
   of God that didn't make sense to me. I've found comfort
   in II Corinthians 5:13-14a. It talks both about the feeling
   of insecurity we have when being a flow through vessel
   for God, as well as our purpose and power in doing so.
   Rephrase it below in your own words.

3.   It takes faith to believe God wants to capture your attention
     and order your steps to meet specific needs. Paraphrase
     these verses in your own words.

        Proverbs 16:9

        Proverbs 21:1

4.   Have you ever felt like the simple things you do don't count
     for much? Paraphrase these verses.

        I Corinthians 1:27

        Psalms 19:7

Verse 15

Verse 16

8. Trying harder leads to frustration, guilt, and hopelessness, whereas trusting more results in joy, anticipation, and a close personal relationship with the God of the universe. Write Jeremiah 17:7-8 in your own words below.

9. Like Madison, do you sometimes feel like God doesn't hear you, or if He does, that He doesn't care? What does Psalms 33:18-22 have as a prerequisite for believing you are being heard and cared for by God?

10. God is closer than your next breath. Write Psalms 145:18 in your own words.

11. According to John 14:6, who does Jesus claim to be?

12. Have you learned to let God lead you around, even when His instructions don't make any sense to your logical mind?" Write Isaiah 55:8-9 in your own words below.

13. God remembered Pam's spiritual birthday, even when I didn't. He sent me to her home to communicate His love. Read Acts 10:20 and 29. What are your thoughts about how God moves people around, even when they don't know why in advance?

Chapter 2. Foundation-Building Analogies

1. Have you ever felt like God expected you to create your own spiritual goodness? Just like faking oxygen production in an emergency would be impossible, faking godliness is even more ludicrous and deadly. Paraphrase II Corinthians 13:5 to understand how to avoid being a spiritual counterfeit.

2. Write II Corinthians 11:13-15 in your own words to grasp God's response to pretenders or to those who want to be a god instead of trusting in Him.

    For further study, read the story of Korah from Numbers 16-17.

3. Read John 5:30 from the Amplified Version of the Bible. How dependent on God was Jesus during His life?

4. It is easy to fear that God will not come through for you. What truth do you find in Hebrews 4:16 for times of terror?

5. Look up Ephesians 5:18 and write it below in your own words. Just how much does God want you to give yourself over to His power and purposes?

6. Remember how, without God, we are like straws stuck in an empty glass: Full of hot air and ready to share? Paraphrase the following verses to help you understand the importance of constant submersion into God.

    II Timothy 2:16

    Philippians 2:3

7. Do you agree that any good deed done without God's directive and energy is vacant of Him? Either way, read the following passages and respond with your thoughts.

Isaiah 64:6

Revelation 3:17

8. Expand on the analogy of corrective lenses as you read these verses. How does godly perspective transform our experience of life from spiritually blurry to clear?

Colossians 2:3

John 1:7

Ephesians 3:9

Hebrews 4:13

9. There is an old adage, "Hurting people hurt people." Others throw their trash at you all the time, intentionally, unintentionally, aware, or unaware. From I Corinthians 13:2, what is the only thing that can help you get out from under the mountain of rubbish?

10. As you yield to God, He promises to bring good out of everything that feels bad in the moment. The worse it feels, the greater the good that will come when you yield to Him by faith. Personalize I Corinthians 15:36 for the next time you face sadness, grief, or loss.

11. When life is just plain confusing, I Corinthians 4:8-12 can help you remember that this, too, shall pass. Paul lived through a lot of tough stuff and came out the other side, feeling loved and cared for by God. Write down some of the trials God brought Paul through.

12. Based on the verses below, how important is it to forgive?

    Matthew 6:15

    Colossians 3:13

Chapter 3. Real-Life Stories to Develop the Dream

1. Worrying, trying harder, and always feeling like you are falling short is the opposite of God's will for your life. God does not want your effort: He wants your love. According to Ephesians 2:8-9, why does God refuse to consider your self-effort as an acceptable peace offering?

2. Read Galatians 3:1-6. From your perspective, what was the #1 mistake being made by these Christians? What was Abraham's exemplary alternative?

3. God apparently feels that being invisible to us is a good thing. He sent Jesus to show us a human rendition of Himself. Write these verses from your own perspective.

I Timothy 1:17

Colossians 1:15

John 1:14

4. We'll cover the 4R Response in greater detail in Chapter 5, but here simply guess the best you can to rank your current level of mastery for each on a scale of one to ten (ten best). Write NS (not sure) if this step is not yet on your radar.

Recognize.
- ❑ I often recognize I'm in trouble.
- ❑ When I realize I'm in trouble, I often seek God for help.
- ❑ When I seek God for help, I employ faith in the process.

Release.
- ❑ I readily release any pain, problems, mental processes, or predicaments to God.
- ❑ I leave them with God, or if I realize I've taken something back, I quickly re-release.

Receive.
- ❑ I habitually quiet myself after release to receive an exchange gift from God.
- ❑ I easily identify whether He is extending peace, hope, comfort, or some other gift.
- ❑ I trust that what I am understanding in these moments is from God and not me.

Respond.
- ❑ Upon receiving the exchange gift God offers, I say a heartfelt "Thank You."
- ❑ After saying thanks, I offer my availability for anything God wants me to do next.

6. You were introduced to five flow through vessels by name and story. Although your life experiences may not precisely mirror any of them, portions of each story may have impacted you. In the spaces below, jot a thought or feeling that emerged while reading each story.

  Marie with her brain aneurysm - _____

  Julie with her wayward husband - _____

  Tom with his perpetual health issues - _____

  Cheryl with her handicapped child - _____

  Laura with her unaccepted apology - _____

7. I paraphrase Titus 3:5 like this, "I need God! I don't have enough money, good works, or personal purity to buy my way into a relationship with God. He knows it. He planned for it. He extended forgiveness toward me so I could come to Him clean, fresh, and perfect, because of Jesus and what the Holy Spirit has done in my life." That's the Marnie Version (MV). Read it from the Bible and write it in your words below.

8. The flow through examples in this chapter shared two
   things in common: 1) Each was drowning in excruciating
   pain, and 2) chose to call on Jesus. Paraphrase Acts 4:12 in
   light of this choice.

9. From Matthew 28:18, identify why the name of Jesus is the
   most powerful response.

10. Calling on the name of Jesus is like a spiritual crisis, 911
    number. Can you see why from Philippians 2:9-11?

I find it interesting that the reference, Philippians 2:9-11
is similar to 911 and that Americans called on God after
terrorists brought us to our knees on 9/11. All things need
not be coincidence when one believes in a God.

Chapter 4. Hang On for the Ride of Your Life

1. Living through a wild ride, whether emotionally or at an
    amusement park, triggers emotions. The book of Acts in
    the Bible is like a story-book version of the early church,
    including some graphic descriptions of emotionally charged
    experiences. Read the featured verses below and write the
    emotion you'd expect to feel if you were in that situation.
    Afterward, read the rest of the story.

    >   Paul. Acts 14:19. _____
    >   Now read the rest of the story in Acts 14:20 and write your
    >   thoughts below.

    >   Peter. Acts 12:4. _____
    >   Now read the rest of the story in Acts 12:5-10 and com-
    >   ment below.

2. We always want God to rescue us in obvious ways, like he
    did for Paul and Peter, but God doesn't always do that. The
    following stories are messy.

    a. Read the story in Acts 7:54-60. If you'd been Stephen,
       what emotion would you have felt in verse 56?

b. Read the story in Genesis 22. If you'd been Abraham, what emotion would you have felt in verses 11-12?

c. Read the story in Daniel 6. If you'd been Daniel, what emotion would you have felt in verse 22?

3. Read Hebrews 11:32-40. These God-lovers all lived prior to the cross of Christ. Imagine being in the situation of each person. What prayer would you be shooting at God? It says, "None of these people got what they were promised." Why would God make them wait? Paraphrase verses 39-40 as you understand them.

4. While we all suffer due to the existence of evil on earth, a Christian's suffering need not be without benefit, and, during the trials, God never leaves us without help.

    Read II Corinthians 11:24-27 and rephrase your perspective of God's thoughts from verse 29.

    Read it another way in II Corinthians 4:6-10, then describe the godly perspective from verses 15-18.

5. We are going to face suffering, with or without God's help. Our choice is whether to go through hardships with Him, for His glory, or alone. Paraphrase I John 3:16 in your own words.

6. It is often during times of extreme pain, stress, sadness, or confusion that we do things we later regret. Express God's comfort from Proverbs 28:13.

7. After especially grievous sins, you may fear God will give up on you.

    What do you see in Isaiah 43:25?

    What comfort can you find in Psalms 103:12-17?

8. Getting on a roller coaster ride that has a track record of killing riders would be foolish at best, deadly at worst. Buckling up with God can feel scary, until you get to know Him. Why do you feel God calls us to extreme faith, as described in Hebrews 11:6?

Chapter 5. How to Move Beyond Drama, Trauma & Self-Induced Stress

1. As children of God, our first response when in trouble should be to call on God. There are over 40 verses in Psalms alone about calling on His name. The third commandment is, "You shall not take the name of the Lord your God in vain." Compare how our culture typically uses God's name (casually, as a curse word, and so on), compared with God's idea of appropriate usage.

2. God gave 10 commandments and over 600 laws in the Old Testament, plus over 1000 commands in the New Testament, and every single one is for the benefit of you or someone else God loves. Can you identify any drama, trauma, or stress that could have been avoided in your life if you had obeyed God's rules?

3. Here I'm going to give you a new word picture that simplifies the 4R Response even further. Below is a board with two sections: Above the line, "God's Stuff" and below the line, "My Stuff."

In this exercise, God's stuff includes things like world peace, the US economy, heaven, and other things that are obviously outside my ability to affect.

Below the line, in the "My Stuff" space, I write things I usually take responsibility for including deciding what to wear, paying bills, and so on—things I personally oversee or do.

Here's the deal: God wants the entire bottom half of that slate, my half, completely EMPTY except for Him. I know that sounds impossible, but it's your first step toward experiential freedom in Christ.

Whenever you find yourself becoming emotionally involved with something, recognize that it's on the wrong half of the board: It's on your side while it should be on God's. Mentally, spiritually, and emotionally, lift it by faith to God—releasing it up to Him.

Let go of it completely, like you gave the keys to the new owner, and then ask if there's anything God wants you to do for Him—related or unrelated to the issue you just released—because that's no longer your problem.

Experiment with this and write some observations below. (Do not be surprised if it feels very "irresponsible" to release your concerns to God. We are all addicted to the delusion that we are in control of anything!)

4.   This chapter focused on the 4Rs. The first R is recognize. It's easy to see we're in trouble, but not so easy to remember we need God. Review Revelations 3:17 and then rephrase Galatians 5:16 to help you remember your desperate need for God.

5.   The second R is to release your troubles, wild emotions, or difficult situations to God. Rephrase I Peter 5:7 below.

6. The third R is to receive. God is a generous gift-giver. Are you experiencing His blessings? Rephrase John 16:24 in your own words.

7. The fourth R is to respond with a "Thank You" after which you offer your assistance. Remember, most of us skip the second R, wanting to "fix it" ourselves. Write James 4:6 in your own words to show how God feels about our independence, and James 4:10 to reveal the outcome of doing things God's way.

8. Pride doesn't always look boastful, sometimes it's an invisible thought process. Paraphrase Proverbs 16:18.

9. Look up Proverbs in the Amplified Version (AMP) of the Bible. What is the word that comes immediately before the word "fool" every single time?

10. The next time you feel distant from God, try humbling yourself enough to remember how much you need Him. Rephrase Psalms 8:4 to realize the amazing opportunity you have to be loved by God.

11. Have you ever wondered if you need to thank God "for" hard circumstances? I've come to believe that we will eventually thank Him for everything—when we see it all from His perspective. In the interim, take comfort as you paraphrase God's instructions from I Thessalonians 5:18.

12. It will take time and focused energy to develop a deep dependence on God. One of the best ways I know how to move toward that goal is to learn, personalize, and become a master at the 4Rs. Read my rendition of I John 5:3, then read it from your Bible and write it in your own words below.

"My desire is to experience the true love of God flowing through my life as I am learning to do life God's way. It will never come naturally to me, but with practice, I'll receive it supernaturally as my habitual response. Those who have already learned and mastered the simple skills of calling on God find His ways neither irksome, burdensome, oppressive, or unreasonable. Quite the opposite. They habitually experience God's love flowing through their lives." Marnie's Version (MV)

Chapter 6. Stop Being Abused By Life & Start Being Used by God

1. During Amah-El Club, I learned the humble phrase, "God, I don't have enough _____ for so-and-so just now. I need some of Yours. Thank You." Personalize this sentiment and use it at some point this week. Journal your experience below.

2. After the story about the pan of dessert falling upside-down on the floor, I wrote, "I can't always say, 'I would have done it that way,' but I can always say, 'God was here.'" Rephrase Proverbs 3:5-6 as it relates to times when you cannot understand why God would allow something to happen the way it did.

3. Years ago, while reading Psalms 91, I began meditating on
    a phrase from verse 14 which says, "I [God] will set him on
    high, because he knows My name."

At the time, I knew many names for God, but I made it my
goal to find more. My initial research uncovered nearly 300
which I organized alphabetically. One day while shampoo-
ing our pastor's carpets, a tune came into my head along
with a few names near the beginning of the list. As more
came, I kept turning off the machine to jot down the next
names and before long, "The Name Song" had been written. It's now on my "It's My Honor" CD and sung around
the world. Below are the names from that song.

Read through the poem that I put to music, and highlight
a few names that stand out to you today. Next, do a Bible
search of your own to find at least one verse in which each
of your highlighted names appears. Write the reference in
the open space at right.

> Accessible, Advocate, Almighty King
> Alpha, Omega, Amen.
> The Author and Finisher of my faith,
> My Banner, the Beginning, the End.
>
> My Beloved, my Bridegroom, the Bread of Life
> Bright and Morning Star.
> My Consolation, Compassionate Friend
> Gift of God sent from heaven afar.

Comforter, Confidence, Consuming Fire,
Day Star, Deliverer, Lord,
Defender of widows and orphans poor
Refuge, Stronghold, the Wide Open Door.

Counselor, Christ Child, Good Teacher and Friend,
Faithful, God with us, Our Guide.
My Helper, Hope, Hiding Place, Infinite Judge,
My Physician, You're always by my side.

Holy Spirit, Immutable, God Only Wise,
Jealous, Jehovah, Just One.
King of King, Lord of Lords, Light of Life,
Living Bread, Lamb of God, Great I Am.

Man of Sorrows, yet Master, the Most Holy One
Merciful, Gracious and Pure.
Messiah, Omnipotent, Mighty to Save
Perfect Passover, Providence Sure.

Omnipresent, Invisible, Most Powerful Love,
Providence, Radiant Star.
Sinless, Sin-bearer, my Surety
Unspeakable Gift, Lord You are.

My Salvation, Righteousness, Redeemer and Rock
Unsearchable Wisdom, All Peace
Which is and which was and which is to come
True Teacher, Humble Servant, High Priest.

Chorus:
Name above all names, ever the same,
Name above all names, on my face I fall,
My mouth's filled with Your praise,
Your holy name I raise,
I cannot be quiet, I must not be still,
My mind joins emotion, emotion joins will,
You set me on high when I honor Your name,
Oh, God, Your name I proclaim.

4. There are 15 items listed in the "Uniqueness of You" section. Were any of these new to you? Read Psalms 139:13-18, exploring the reality that God formed you, every detail of who you know yourself to be, purposefully.

5. You took a flow through self-test earlier. Besides bringing God pleasure, what are His two goals for your life from Psalms 119:73-74?

6. Remembering the dolphin analogy, paraphrase I Thessalonians 5:17.

7. What does I Thessalonians 5:16 teach is the best way to enjoy your new dolphin-style life?

8. We are to enjoy life on earth, as much as possible, with our heart focused on God and heaven. An incredible truth is that we have the opportunity to take stuff with us into heaven. Read and personalize I Corinthians 3:11-15.

9. Many people are counting many ways to get into God's heaven. According to Galatians 2:16, what is the entrance ticket God will accept?

10. In Chapter 4, I asked if you'd ever officially gotten things right with God by trusting Jesus Christ as your Savior from sin. If you weren't sure about it then, are you ready now? Paraphrase Ephesians 2:4-7 to understand more deeply how God feels about you.

Chapter 7. Move Forward One Step at a Time

1. Be honest with yourself and God (He knows anyway): What is one habit that has driven you crazy for a long time now? Maybe you have tried everything: fasting, prayer, detoxification, accountability, or you name it, and still, the habit or addiction persists.

2. In Exodus and Joshua, God tells the people to take the land gradually instead of all at once. It's the same with habit replacement. Personalize these verses as they apply.

    Exodus 23:29

II Corinthians 10:5

3. "Walking with God is a relationship, not a religion. Brush your teeth religiously, but love God relationally." Paraphrase Hebrews 10:11 in your own words.

4. When you messed up as a child, were you corrected or punished? Correction includes love, forgiveness, and reasonable consequences. Punishment is based on judgment, does not necessarily include love, and can be very harsh. Is it possible that you punish your adult self in an attempt to get your behavior under control? Write out Romans 2:4 to get a glimpse into God's plan.

5. Our English word for "love" has four meanings in the original text. "Agape" love refers to God's kind of love. It can only be obtained directly from God. The other three loves, eros (sexual), storge (motherly), and phileo (friendship) love, can be done with human effort.

    a. Read I Corinthians 13:4-8, replacing the words "love" or "charity" first with God's name.

    b. Reread it, this time replacing them with your name, because, as God's flow through vessel, this can be you!

    c. Now read verses 1-3 to see how life feels when lived without God's Agape love.

6. It's one thing to not "rock the boat," and another to get out of the boat and walk on the water. That's exactly what Peter did. Read Matthew 14:25-33 and write down Peter's habitual behavior when on water, compared to what he could do with God's help flowing through.

7. Proverbs 13:11 is talking about money, but there are many types of wealth. I view freedom as wealth, too. How does this verse relate to habit replacement?

8. Trusting God is choosing to act in utter dependence on Him, while trying harder is opting to retain control. From Galatians 3:3, what is our motivation for resisting the invitation to fully trust Him?

Chapter 8. Learn to Appreciate the Amazing Process of Habit Formation

1. It's interesting to me how God "appears" to set people up for failure, while bringing astounding good out of their lives. The story of King Solomon always amazes me. God invited him to ask for anything he wanted in the world. He could have asked for wealth, power, health, or fame, but Solomon chose wisdom.

    Delighted by this selfless choice, God proceeded to bless Solomon with wisdom *plus* the rest—riches, fame, and power. Solomon, in response, attempted to enjoy all that good stuff without God. The gift replaced the Giver as the love of his life.

    I've written the Marnie Version (MV) of some verses below. Write them from your Bible, in your own words, to experience how it must have felt to have everything—everything except the only thing that matters, friendship with God.

    > Ecclesiastes 1:1 MV. Honestly, without God, life, even at its best, is ridiculous.

Ecclesiastes 2:17 MV. Life without God in control is awful! Work is hateful, hard, and empty. No matter how hard I work, it's not worth it!

Ecclesiastes 12:13-14 MV. There is only one conclusion I can reach after spending my life looking for satisfaction outside of God: God is the answer! God knows everything, sees everything, and is all that matters.

2. The fiery furnace will prove that anything done without God is eternally worthless, even if it seemed helpful in the moment. Read Ecclesiastes 2:25. Solomon was the wisest, richest, most powerful man in the world, yet he couldn't find joy without God. Why would you think you could ever be happy without God in your life?

3. If you've been doing things independent of God, are you ready to think about them from God's perspective? Paraphrase II Corinthians 5:17 in your own words.

4. The picture of being surrounded by a jail cell of pasta strands may seem silly, but the Bible tells us exactly what we need to do to get free. I've rephrased the following verses into the Marnie Version. Look them up in your Bible and add your own paraphrase below.

Romans 15:13 MV. I can trust God completely and move into freedom in His time and way, all the while overflowing with His Spirit for the benefit of others.

Romans 6:22 MV. I am free! I am free to love God with my whole heart.

John 8:32 MV. There is no hiding or pretending involved in the freedom I have in Christ.

5. It can be confusing! While sin has no place in a Christian's life, every Christian I've ever known sins. Let's walk through a few passages to help clarify God's perspective on sinning saints.

    a. As Christians, we sin. What is the comfort you find in I John 2:1-2?

    b. I John 3:9 says it is "not possible" for someone who is born of God to commit sin, yet we know we do. One idea is that God has so thoroughly forgiven our sins that, from His perspective, they do not exist, even when they do. This is not blindness, it is a choice to cover sin with love. How does I John 4:10 relate to this fact?

c. I John 1:8-9 says it's critically important for us to recognize and confess our sin. Since God has already forgiven
us, why do you think the Holy Spirit brings sin to our
attention, in the form of convicting thoughts?

d. Romans 8:1 assures us that God is not condemning us for
our sins. As far as He's concerned, once we are under the
umbrella of Christ's blood, it's as if we'd never sinned. It's
over; it's a non-issue. Paraphrase Romans 8:1 below with
your name it.

e. When you feel condemnation (which, like punishment, is
loveless), what can you do with those thoughts based on
I John 3:20?

f. Jesus has completely, once and for all—past, present and future—taken care of our sin issue with God. Write Hebrews 4:14-16 in your own words below.

For further study, read Romans 6-8.

Chapter 9. Get Unstuck ASAP

1. Feeling stuck can feel awful! Psalms 131 uses the analogy of a mother comforting a small baby. Write it as it relates to God rocking your soul safely as He frees you from your entrapments in His time and way.

2. Have you ever been in a ditch, waiting for a tow truck, wondering if it would ever arrive? Write II Peter 3:8-9 as it relates to the timing of your freedom from any habit or addiction.

3. Sometimes we stay stuck because we are convinced God could never forgive us for our latest misdeeds. How did Peter feel in Luke 5:8? Compare it to what God said about him in Matthew 16:18.

4. One of the most famous Bible verses is Romans 8:28, but most people never read the verse after it, which explains what the popular verse means. The passage uses the analogy of a potter molding clay. Read Romans 8:28-29 and write below the part of verse 29 that identifies the good God promises to bring out of even the worst trouble.

5. We want results when and how we want them! Read Isaiah 45:9. Who is the potter? Who is the clay?

6. Patience is a virtue, and if you are desperately waiting for an answer to a prayer that feels intensely important to you, use the 4Rs right now to release your impatience to God. Write a prayer under each of the 4Rs below.

> **Recognize.** I recognize that I've been demanding You to respond in my time about _____. (Write a current struggle below.)
>
>
>
>
> **Release.** I release my _____ along with my desire for immediate gratification in this area. (Write below any negative emotions associated with the struggle you mentioned above.)
>
>
>
>
>
> **Receive.** I am listening. What do you want to give me right now in exchange for my continual begging for this need? I'll listen until you tell me. (Write it below.)

Respond. Thank You! I understood _____ (answer from #3). Now, is there anything I can do for You about my request, or anything else? You name it, I'm on it! (Write what you think you are supposed to do below.)

7. In the previous chapter, we learned that God has forgiven our sins so completely that, from His perspective, our sin is not a dividing factor (unless we hide, protect, or lie about it). Read the verses below and write beside each an action you can take when a godless habit shows up with its prison bars, preventing you from intimacy with your Creator.

Isaiah 59:2

I John 1:9

Isaiah 40:31

8. Complete honesty with ourselves and God, combined with faith in His loving forgiveness, is the key to experiencing freedom from any bondage. Read Psalms 139:1-12 and then paraphrase verses 23-24 below.

9. No matter what the habit, you can actually replace it with a better one—the habit of God dependence. Paraphrase this sentiment from Psalms 119:71.

10. Even if you stay stuck for a while longer, what does Psalms 16:8 promise when you apply the focus of Psalms 73:26?

11. Jesus poured the wine, then poured out His blood for us. He now offers to flow through us. Write John 7:38 in your own words.

12. "While abstinence is often a necessary step on the road toward freedom, it is not always God's ultimate goal for you.... God's goal for you is not that you will forever and ever want to go back to your old, default responses, needing abstinence to avoid them, but that you will learn to hate sin and never want to do it again. Herein lies freedom." Personalize Galatians 5:1 below.

13. Prior to full freedom, expect God to prompt you to take preventative precautions. He is, after all, your loving Parent who does not want you to suffer unnecessarily. Rephrase these verses as they apply.

Matthew 26:41

Proverbs 4:26

I Corinthians 10:12

14. Every morning, as I'm putting on my physical clothes, I'm also putting on my spiritual clothes. I have found this discipline to be invaluable (and go into it in greater detail in my book, *Feeling Loved: Connecting with God in the Minutes You Have*).

Here, in an attempt to convince you to adopt it as part of *your* morning routine, I'll share my own process. First, I put up the shield of faith, and then I use the children's ditty, "Head and shoulders, knees and toes," to help me remember the rest. In my heart, and in communion with God, I prayerfully:

- Take up the shield of faith
- Strap on the helmet of salvation
- Put on the breastplate of righteousness
- Buckle on the belt of truth
- Tie on the shoes of peace

I then pick up the Sword of the Lord after which I keep on praying—all day. I just keep breathing the air of prayer.

This is, of course, a grave oversimplification of an awesome spiritual opportunity that I hope you'll explore and adopt as your own.

As part of contemplating its necessity, or launching this as a new habit in your life, take time right now to read Ephesians 6:13-18. Can you envision yourself suiting up in spiritual armor each morning? If so, what's your first, best guess at how you'd go about it?

Marnie Swedberg

15. Prior to the list of spiritual armor, Ephesians 6:13 says, "And, having done all, stand." There will be times when God will ask you to stand firm in the face of a temptation. Jesus experienced this when, after 40 days with no food, He was tempted by Satan with nowhere to run and nowhere to hide. In His physically, emotionally, and relationally emaciated condition, Jesus was able to overcome. He used the principle of resisting without resisting. I like to call it persistent, non-resistance. Explore the following verses and express how God wants to enable you to behave in similar situations.

Exodus 14:13

Psalms 18:33

Nehemiah 6:11

I Corinthians 16:13

James 4:7

I Peter 5:9

16. Finally, there are times when we are *not* to stand still, but to run. Personalize these verses using your own name in the instructions.

II Timothy 2:22-24

I Corinthians 6:18

I Corinthians 10:14

I Timothy 6:11

Chapter 10. Identifying God's Presence In Your Past

1. God is not like your dad! Whether you had a great dad, a
   bad dad, or an absentee dad, God is far greater than any
   human dad. The role of a dad is to model godly behavior,
   but most fail horribly at this task. Ephesians 6:4 documents
   a common flaw shared by most dads. Write it below.

2. God is not like your boss! Write the portion of Ephesians 6:9 describing the common shortcomings of most bosses.

3. God is love. Zephaniah 3:17 is a little love song from God to you. How does this verse make you feel?

4. Go back to Daniel 6, where God spared Daniel from the lions. Verse 24 explains that, after pulling Daniel out of the den, the king had all his accusers, along with their families, thrown in. It says, "before they reached the bottom of the den, the lions had overpowered them and had broken their bones in pieces." Write I Peter 5:8 in your own words and explain why a good God would want you to invest full faith in Him.

5. Opportunistic faith is a start, but it's unhealthy. Read Acts 5:1-10, Acts 19:13-16, and Amos 5:21 to discover how the spiritual realm perceives people who attempt to "use God" instead of be used by Him.

6. Using God as a consultant sets you up for faithless actions. Read I Samuel 28:5-7 and journal below a time you remember calling out to God for help, and then, when He didn't instantly respond, running off to find some other solution.

7. In Judges 6:36-40, we find Gideon testing God. In Judges 7:9-11, another 911, God offers Gideon an extra proof of His direction, without Gideon needing to ask. When we sincerely want to do God's will, but are confused, afraid, or unclear about something, God honors a testing heart. In fact, Malachi 3:10 instructs us to test Him in certain things. Deuteronomy 6:16 tells us not to test the Lord like the people did at Massah. Read Exodus 17:7 and write below the type of testing God abhors.

8. There are so many Bible characters who displayed full
    faith in God. I love the response of the three Hebrew boys
    who were about to be thrown into a fiery furnace due to
    their outspoken faith in God. Read and personalize their
    response from Daniel 3:17-18 as it applies to a concern or
    fear you are facing today.

9. When you are afraid, run to God. Paraphrase I John 4:18,
    remembering that the word "love" here refers to God's
    agape love.

10. Reread Matthew 5:14. It takes courage to share your faith
    in God with others. From Acts 26:17, why would you do it
    despite the fear?

Chapter 11. Possibility Thinking with God

1. Possibility thinking can be threatened when we feel accused or afraid. Write a phrase about each of the following verses explaining why we should be legitimately terrified of God.

    Jeremiah 5:22-24

    I Chronicles 16:25-26

    Psalms 76:7-8

    Psalms 96:4-5

2. Once having come to God through Jesus, fear shifts from
    guilty to reverent. Godly fear is good. Personalize these
    verses to put the fear of God into perspective.

    Deuteronomy 6:24

    Psalms 30:3-4

    Psalms 111:10

    Romans 8:15

    Psalms 56:3-4

3. Psalms 23 is one of the most beloved passages in the Bible due to its picturesque representation of how the Shepherd, Jesus Christ, cares for His sheep, including you.

    Paraphrase Psalms 23:4-5 as it relates to your need to trust Him fully no matter what your circumstances.

    Children are constantly asking, begging, and trying to get adults to give them stuff. They are focused on getting whatever it is they see that seems good to them. Write Psalms 23:1 as it relates to maturing in your requests, paying close attention to the use of the word "want."

4. Job went through the worst possible scenario, losing practically everything within hours: his children, wealth, health, and hope. Job pleased God with his response when he said, "I came into the world naked, I'll leave it with nothing. The Lord gave, the Lord has taken away; blessed be the name of the Lord." Job 1:21, MV. What are your thoughts in response to Job 1:22 and 42:12-17?

5. The Bible is a compilation of three-quarter million words, 31,000 verses, 1,100 chapters, and 66 books that God flowed through men, to help you understand His love and provision for you. Review these verses and write your thoughts after each.

    Romans 15:4

    Hebrews 4:12

6. Ezekiel 16:1-13 is a word picture of God's extravagant love toward you. Verses 14-63 depict a spurned God. Again, if you are outside the covering grace of Jesus' blood, be afraid! Write your response to Ezekiel 16 below.

Chapter 12. The Rest of Your Story

1. In Isaiah 66:1, God says that heaven is His home. In addition to getting to live in the presence of God, rephrase the description of heaven found in Revelation 21:4 to describe some other differences between heaven and earth.

2. Have you ever been away from home so long that you got homesick? Maybe you missed the people, or possibly you longed for the comforts of home. Heaven is your real home. Rephrase Philippians 3:20 in your own words.

3. God is outside of time. Write Isaiah 46:10 as you understand it.

4. God already knows when you will leave planet Earth. Paraphrase Psalms 139:16 in light of this reality.

5. From Colossians 3:1-4, why should you be heavenly minded while you are here on earth?

6. Read I Peter 4:7-11. In light of heaven, how should we live now?

7. Hebrews 12:1-2 assure us that God-lovers who've passed on are watching our lives with a tremendous level of comfort and confidence due to their eternal perspective. Think of a godly person you knew who is already with Jesus. What do you think they'd be saying to you right now if you could hear them cheering you on?

8. One of my favorite quotes is, "There is time to do every-thing God wants me to do." The first song I ever wrote was based on Psalms 31:15a, "My times are in Your hands." As you read the poetry below, open your heart to God and His plans for your life—for time, and eternity.

> My times are in your hand, O Lord, I trust You.
> My days, my hours, my minutes, Yours, they're Your due.
>
> Chorus:
> What could be so important? That I'd wander from Your plan.
> You left mansions and heaven, to save me as I am.
>
> My schedule to Your loving will, I submit.
> All the deeds I'm meant to do, You'll permit.
>
> My great ambitions, my hopes, my dreams, at Your feet.
> Only as I lay them there, Your will meet.
>
> Ending:
> I seem able to find the time
> To do the things I really want to do.
> But yielding all my rights is how,
> I trust You!

9.   During times of confusion or pain, I've adopted this motto and mindset: "I choose to be as thankful in this moment as I will be when I meet Jesus face-to-face and understand everything He is doing right now to help me, protect me, and provide for me." Rephrase these verses in your own words.

Hebrews 12:28

Psalms 46:1

10. God's choices for us can be confusing! Most days the eye-witness accounts report Jesus healing all the people who came to Him. Yet one day, at the Pool of Bethesda, He chose to heal just one man, leaving the rest of the invalids lying in their pain and helplessness. Read II Corinthians 12:7-10. If God chooses to make you wait for an answer to prayer, do you feel you might be able to give Him the benefit of the doubt and trust Him with that?

11. Read Acts 9:36-42. What if it's the other way around and God chooses to heal someone through you? Maybe He wants to do miracles through your life. Would you be willing to let Him flow that through you, too?

‘

12. Write down a few of your favorite go-to phrases from the chapter. After that, as often as possible, share as many as you adopt with the group at www.FlowThroughVessel.com.

Appendices

Appendix I
Scripture Index

*T*he following Scriptures are referred to in this book.

Acts 4:12	Hebrews 12:1-2	Isaiah 43:25	Proverbs 16:9
Acts 5:1-10	Hebrews 12:28	Isaiah 45:9	Proverbs 16:18
Acts 7:54-60	Hebrews 13:5	Isaiah 46:10	Proverbs 18:10
Acts 9:36-42	I Chronicles 16:25-26	Isaiah 55:8-9	Proverbs 21:1
Acts 10:20-29	I Corinthians 1:27	Isaiah 59:2	Proverbs 28:13
Acts 12:4-10	I Corinthians 3:11-15	Isaiah 64:6	Psalms 8:4
Acts 14:19-20	I Corinthians 4:6-18+A104	Isaiah 66:1	Psalms 18:33
Acts 14:22	I Corinthians 6:18	James 4:6-10	Psalms 19:7
Acts 15:32	I Corinthians 10:12	James 4:7	Psalms 23
Acts 19:13-16	I Corinthians 10:14	Jeremiah 5:22-24	Psalms 30:3-4
Acts 27:16	I Corinthians 13:1-8	Jeremiah 17:7-8	Psalms 31:15a
Amos 5:21	I Corinthians 15:36	Job 1:21	Psalms 33:18-22
Colossians 1:15	I Corinthians 16:13	Job 1:22	Psalms 46:1
Colossians 2:3	I John 1:8-10	Job 42:12-17	Psalms 46:10
Colossians 3:1-4	I John 2:1-2	John 1:7	Psalms 56:3-4

Colossians 3:13	I John 3:9	John 1:14	Psalms 73:26
Colossians 3:24	I John 3:16	John 3:3	Psalms 76:7-8
Colossians 4:7	I John 3:20	John 4:36-38	Psalms 91
Daniel 3:17-18	I John 4:4	John 5:30	Psalms 96:4-5
Daniel 6	I John 4:10	John 7:38	Psalms 103:12-17
Deuteronomy 6:16	I John 4:18	John 8:32	Psalms 111:10
Deuteronomy 6:24	I John 5:3	John 14:6	Psalms 119:71
Ecclesiastes 1:1	I Kings 17:7-16	John 16:8	Psalms 119:73-74
Ecclesiastes 2:17	I Peter 4:7-11	John 16:24	Psalms 131
Ecclesiastes 2:25	I Peter 5:7-8	Judges 6:36-40	Psalms 138:6
Ecclesiastes 12:13-14	I Peter 5:9	Judges 7:9-11	Psalms 139:1-24
Ephesians 2:4-7	I Samuel 28:5-7	Luke 5:8	Psalms 145:18-19
Ephesians 2:8-9	I Thessalonians 5:16-18	Luke 16:10	Revelations 3:17
Ephesians 3:9	I Timothy 1:7	Malachi 3:10	Revelations 21:4
Ephesians 5:18	I Timothy 1:17	Matthew 5:13-16	Romans 1:1
Ephesians 6:4-9	I Timothy 6:11	Matthew 6:15	Romans 2:4
Ephesians 6:13-18	II Corinthians 1:4	Matthew 14:25-33	Romans 6-8
Ephesians 6:22	II Corinthians 4:6-10	Matthew 16:18	Romans 6:18-22
Exodus 14:13	II Corinthians 5:13-14a	Matthew 22:1	Romans 8:1
Exodus 17:7	II Corinthians 5:17	Matthew 26:41	Romans 8:15
Exodus 23:29	II Corinthians 10:5	Matthew 28:18	Romans 8:26
Ezekiel 16:1-13	II Corinthians 11:13-15	Nehemiah 6:11	Romans 8:28
Galatians 1:!1	II Corinthians 11:24-29	Numbers 16-17	Romans 8:29
Galatians 2:16	II Corinthians 12:7-10	Philippians 2:3	Romans 12:2
Galatians 3:1-6	II Corinthians 13:5	Philippians 2:9-11	Romans 14:22
Galatians 5:1	II Peter 3:8-9	Philippians 3:20	Romans 15:4
Galatians 5:16	II Timothy 2:16	Philippians 4:6-7	Romans 15:13
Genesis 22:11-12	II Timothy 2:22-24	Proverbs 3:5-6	Romans 16:25
Hebrews 4:12-16	II Timothy 3:16	Proverbs 4:26	Titus 1:10
Hebrews 11:6	II Timothy 4:22	Proverbs 11:25	Titus 3:5
Hebrews 11:32-40	Isaiah 40:30-31	Proverbs 13:11	Zechariah 3:17

Appendix II
Worksheets

The 4Rs Worksheet

This is the chart to use when you have a "layered" issue, like the day I filled out 23 line items to individually release emotions and concerns to God before coming to peace about the original problem. Sometimes, like a big ball of twine in the mind, you must release several hidden issues in order to be able to fully release the original call to action.

Simply jot down some keywords in each column as you move toward freedom. It only took God and me 15 minutes to get through 23 lines that day, while other times it's taken longer than that to get through one. Don't rush or delay, just do it God's way for that day.

Date	Recognize	Release	Receive	Respond
Keep a record of God's faithfulness.	Be honest about your current situation/pain.	Give it to God as if He's just purchased your car. It's His!	Ask what He'd like to give you as an exchange gift.	Thank Him and ask if there is anything He'd like you to do for Him right now.

Download additional 8.5 x 11 inch blanks at www.FlowThroughVessel.com.

Trust Level Score Sheet

Using the following table, put today's date in the correct box to identify your current trust level with God for each category. Come back and update your score over time. It will be fun to see growth.

	Eternity	Health & Future	Money & Bills	Family & Friends	Daily Needs	Small Stuff
No Confidence						
Opportunistic						
Diplomatic						
Testing						
Sharing						
Fully Confident						

The categories to score include:

Eternity	At what level are you trusting God for what happens to you after you die?
Health	At what level are you trusting God to take care of your physical body now and in the future?
Money	At what level are you trusting God in the area of finances?
People	At what level are you trusting God in your relationships?
Daily Needs	At what level are you trusting God to meet your daily needs?
Small Stuff	At what level are you trusting God when you face small challenges like losing your keys or not knowing how to spend the next 15 minutes?

The level definitions are as follow:

No Confidence in God.	Unawareness of His existence, of who He really is, or that He is available to you personally in this area of your life.
Opportunistic Faith.	Only trusting God when it appears personally beneficial, as a last resort.

Diplomatic Faith.	Assigning God the role of advisor or consultant while retaining all power of attorney. Trusting Him enough for an opinion, but refusing Him any decision-making rights.
Testing Faith.	Flipping faith on and off, exploring the fundamentals of how it works, mostly because it appears in your best interest to do so.
Sharing Faith.	Convinced God is for you and not against you, and willing to ask God to extend His help to those you love. Trusting God because it is in the best interest of others.
Full Confidence.	Trusting, receiving His help, living in gratitude. Internalizing His goodness and marveling at His personal engagement in your everyday life. Yielding to His wishes for Jesus' sake.

Download additional 8.5 x 11 inch blanks at www.FlowThroughVessel.com.

Godly Wealth Roster

This chart helps us comprehend the complexity God faces when deciding how to answer each prayer. When we consider how each answer affects everyone involved and its ripple effect, this chart can increase our trust in this Almighty God and His ability to choose better than we ever could.

Answer options include yes/now or later/no. Add each request to the left side of the chart, then circle how God's answer might affect your character development. You may find that being required to wait, or go without what you are requesting, has the potential to grow far more character than a yes/now answer could.

Use the chart to discover God's intense love and commitment to you, despite His need to say later/no at least some of the time.

Full-size, downloadable versions of this chart are available at www.GodlyWealthExpo.com.

Godly Wealth Analysis

What You See Now

Need, Request, Vision, Dream	Results If Answer Is: Yes / Now	Results If Answer Is: Later / No	Outcomes
	$ C D F G H I J K L N P S T U V W Y	$ C D F G H I J K L N P S T U V W Y	
	$ C D F G H I J K L N P S T U V W Y	$ C D F G H I J K L N P S T U V W Y	
	$ C D F G H I J K L N P S T U V W Y	$ C D F G H I J K L N P S T U V W Y	
	$ C D F G H I J K L N P S T U V W Y	$ C D F G H I J K L N P S T U V W Y	
	$ C D F G H I J K L N P S T U V W Y	$ C D F G H I J K L N P S T U V W Y	
	$ C D F G H I J K L N P S T U V W Y	$ C D F G H I J K L N P S T U V W Y	
	$ C D F G H I J K L N P S T U V W Y	$ C D F G H I J K L N P S T U V W Y	
	$ C D F G H I J K L N P S T U V W Y	$ C D F G H I J K L N P S T U V W Y	
	$ C D F G H I J K L N P S T U V W Y	$ C D F G H I J K L N P S T U V W Y	
	$ C D F G H I J K L N P S T U V W Y	$ C D F G H I J K L N P S T U V W Y	
	$ C D F G H I J K L N P S T U V W Y	$ C D F G H I J K L N P S T U V W Y	
	$ C D F G H I J K L N P S T U V W Y	$ C D F G H I J K L N P S T U V W Y	
	$ C D F G H I J K L N P S T U V W Y	$ C D F G H I J K L N P S T U V W Y	

$ Generosity
C Contentment
D Diligence
F Faithfulness
G Goodness
H Humility
I Kindness
J Joy
K Knowledge
L Love

N Gentleness
P Peace
S Self-Control
T Patience
U Purity
V Forgiveness
W Wisdom
Y Honesty

How to Use this Chart:
1. Enter something you want from God.
2. Circle benefits of a "Yes" or "Now" answer.
3. Circle the benefits of "Later" or "No."
4. Present your request with an open hand.
5. Enter the outcome asap when it's obvious.

Also remember: Timing.
ie - Christmas/Bday Gifts are held
for a particular day. Babies, plants,
etc., have specific gestation periods.

Appendix III
Analogy Index

*T*hroughout this book I've shared numerous analogies. This section includes the page numbers of each so you can easily find the one you are seeking.

Analogy	Page #
Chain	102
Chef	149
Conductor	149
Corrective lenses	23
Dolphins	82
Electrical conduits	20
Embroiderer	149
Garbage truck	26
Heart and lung transplant	97
Hoses	19
Human body	25
Ice cream	119
Inhaler	38
New life	28
Oxygen tube	18
Parent	148
Pasta	124
Physician	115
Pipes	20
Plants	27
Playwright	149
Roller coaster	47
Shed project	116
Sports trainer	122
Straws	21
Tubes	18
Tunnel	50

Appendix IV
How to Connect with Marnie

*M*arnie is available to you 24/7, 365 days a year, as an online mentor through her books, CDs, training programs, boot camps, seminars, and workshops, all of which are included in the mentorship program at www.Marnie.com.

In addition to hosting numerous websites generating millions of hits/year, Marnie Swedberg is the author of 13 books, manages the family restaurant and retail store, hosts her own radio talk show, plus does media and speaking appearances.

Marnie shares her broad experience as she mentors thousands of super busy leaders with her unique approach to being **B.U.S.Y. - Best Unique Strategies for You**. She is fun and fast-paced, yet peaceful and approachable. Her history includes fires, floods, a tornado, car wrecks, business set-backs, a burglary, lightning strike, ambulance rides, cancer in the family, head injury in the family, and more. She models come-back behavior, possibility thinking, and profound faith.

As the webhostess of www.WomenSpeakers.com, the largest online directory of its kind in the world, she connects, influences, and encourages millions of women each year. As the webhostess of www.WomensEvents.info, she promotes major Christian women's events.

As a public speaker, she has presented for large corporations including Honeywell, Prudential, Pillsbury, AT&T, and others; for non-profit groups including Chambers of Commerce, Professional Women's Clubs, public libraries, speaker training conferences, Women of Today, writers conferences, and so on; for Christian women's retreats plus programs for denominations including Baptist, Catholic, Assembly of God, Evangelical Free, Lutheran, and many others.

As a media guest, she hosts her own syndicated radio talk show and has appeared on dozens of TV and radio talk and home shows, plus has been interviewed by newspapers, magazines, blogs, and more. She hosts frequent expos, conferences, and boot camps in addition to the monthly "21 Day Win" Group Coaching program which helps women tackle tough habits from a godly perspective.

Learn more at www.Marnie.com